HOW TO PLAY DRUMS IN 14 DAYS

BY DAVE SCHOEPKE

ISBN: 9798364515537

HOW TO GET THE AUDIO

The audio files for this book are available for free as downloads or streaming on *troynelsonmusic.com*.

We are available to help you with your audio downloads and any other questions you may have. Simply email *help@troynelsonmusic.com*.

See below for the recommended ways to listen to the audio:

Download Audio Files (Zipped)	Stream Audio Files
• Download Audio Files (Zipped)	• Recommended for CELL PHONES & TABLETS
• Recommended for COMPUTERS on WiFi	• Bookmark this page
• A ZIP file will automatically download to the default "downloads" folder on your computer	• Simply tap the PLAY button on the track you want to listen to
• Recommended: download to a desktop/laptop computer *first*, then transfer to a tablet or cell phone	• Files also available for streaming or download at: *soundcloud.com/troynelsonbooks*
• Phones & tablets may need an "unzipping" app such as iZip, Unrar or Winzip	
• Download on WiFi for faster download speeds	

To download the companion audio files for this book, visit: troynelsonmusic.com/audio-downloads/

INTRODUCTION

Hello and welcome to *How to Play Rock Drums in 14 Days*! You may be thinking, "How is it possible to learn rock drums in 14 days?" Well, with a bit of consistent, dedicated practice time and patience, I'm confident that we can get you playing at a beginner level in just two weeks.

There are numerous forms of "rock" music. In this book, the term covers elements of hard rock, country, metal, alternative, EDM, oldies, classic rock, soul, blues, and many other genres and sub-genres. What typically differentiates these styles are the dynamics and sound of the instruments, more so than the actual notes being played. The music that you listen to and enjoy will influence how you incorporate this book into your own playing. However, at the end of each day's lesson, I've included a list of songs for you to listen to and drummers to study so you can discover musical elements and styles beyond what you already know. And, like almost any educator will tell you, approaching these songs and drummers with an open mind is tremendously beneficial, and that goes for any style of music in the world, really. In other words, give 'em a chance. You'll always have your favorites but taking the time to seek out and discover music beyond the radio and your playlists will have you reaping endless rewards as both a player and listener.

HOW TO USE THIS BOOK

The premise of this book is to practice 90 minutes per day for 14 days (they don't need to be consecutive) and, at the end of that time, you'll have advanced your knowledge of and skills in the world of rock drumming.

This book contains quite a bit of content, so please understand that it may take you more than 14 days to get through it confidently, and that's OK! One of the things I have learned as a drum instructor and educator is that every student moves at their own pace. Although this book is laid out so that the difficulty level increases as you progress, the things that snag you up and require more attention may be different from what another person experiences. Regardless, try not to look around and compare yourself to others; instead, look inward, at yourself, your journey, and your goals. By doing so, you'll achieve your goals more easily and enjoy the process along the way.

Some points about the book layout and plan:

- Before you embark on the "14 Day" part of this book, I have included some beginner reading exercises that you can practice on a single drum or pad. These exercises will prepare you for the music you'll encounter in the book.

- For some exercises, I suggest alternate ways to approach them to aid your internalization of the content and ability to express your ideas.

- It's really important that you count your way through every exercise. While it's easy to play an exercise the way you "think" it should be played, I want to discourage you from that approach because it will ultimately extend the process, making it much more difficult on you and your ability to comprehend the material. Instead, take the time to go slow and be accurate in your reading. By doing so, you'll quickly hear the ideas and be able to play them from memory and, in turn, break away from having to read all the time.

- Spend your time away from the drums listening to the music I have recommended and also think about the material you're studying/practicing when you're doing other tasks, like mowing the lawn, doing dishes, taking a shower, or whatever else falls into that sort of activity. By doing so, you'll begin to internalize the material and recall it much quicker the next time you sit down at the kit.

- Review the previous day's material before moving on to the next. If that means placing more time between lessons, then so be it. Just be sure not to look at it in negative light. Remember, the 14-day plan can happen in any way that works best for you and your life.

- There is a lifetime of learning and fulfillment ahead of you. Enjoy the journey that is music and the riches it can afford you, including connecting to a deeper place. Study with a teacher, or many different teachers, and pick their brains!

- Seek out like-minded folks with whom you can play music that you enjoy. This is the last bit of this process that cannot be skipped. The joy of the communion of music is one that has to be experienced, and you'll get that when you get together with others to make music! Let's get rocking!

BASIC MUSIC READING

If you can already read music, then skip this section and get right into Day 1. However, if you're new to reading, or you need a refresher, this section will get you on track with the forthcoming content in this book.

All the patterns in this section are to be played as single-line exercises but could certainly be played in succession without stopping, which is great reading practice. Make sure you go slow and count, being sure to strike the notes when you see them and waiting the appropriate amount of time when you rest. Counting will enable you to be accurate. Never guess! Also, switch hands with each note so that you do not favor a particular hand. Once you get past the first four lines, you can start working on the material in Day 1.

DRUM NOTATION KEY

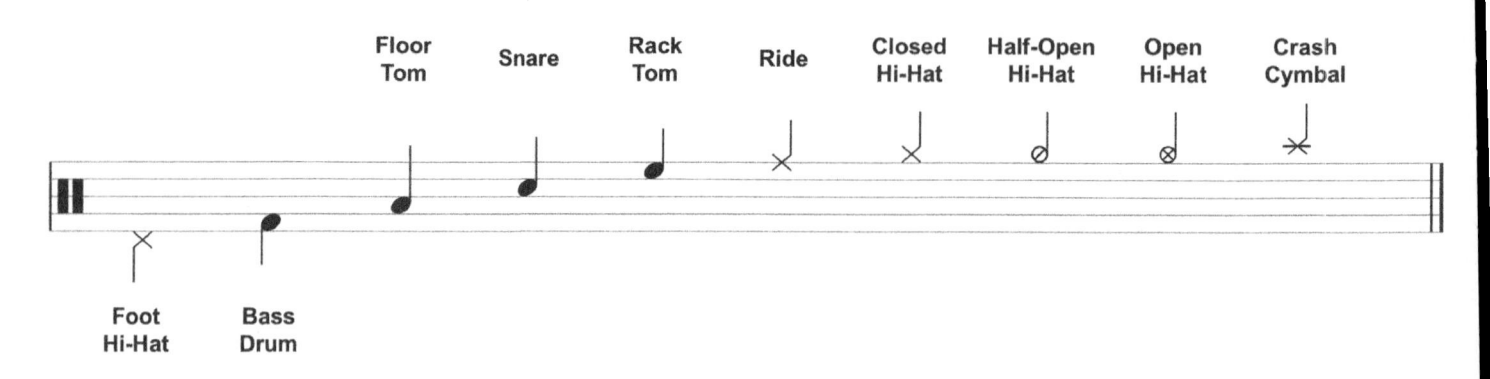

RHYTHM PRIMER

Here's a breakdown of the rhythms that you'll encouter throughout the book, as well as how to count them.

Quarter Notes

Eighth Notes

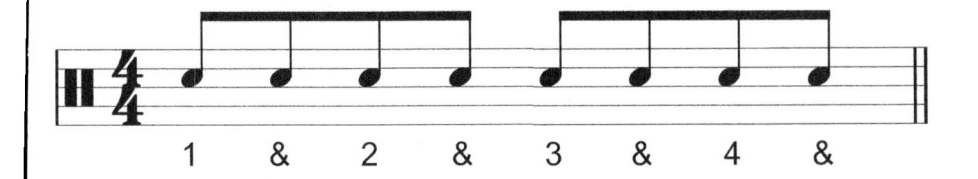

16th Notes

Eighth-Note Triplets

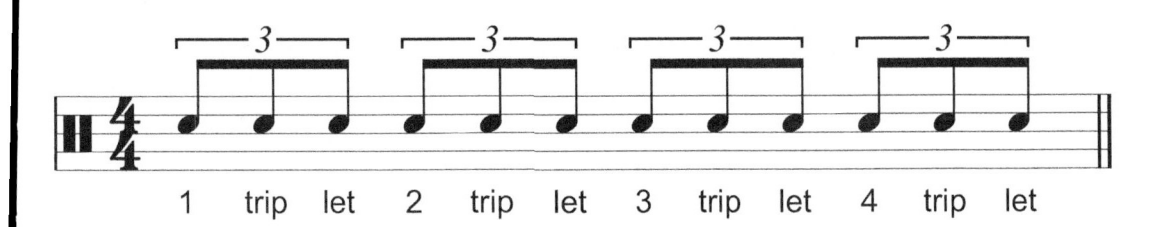

Sextuplets & 16th-Note Triplets

SNARE LINES

Line 1

Quarter notes and eighth notes. Be sure to count "1-and, 2-and, 3-and, 4-and" throughout each measure, even when you're resting. This will help you understand that some notes are longer than others and also prevent you from rushing when you're not playing (since drums have very little controlled sustain, it's easy to do). By counting the entire measure, down to the smallest note, you're accounting for all the possible places you may strike. This will also help you to internalize the time.

Line 2

Go slow and count.

Line 3

Again, go slow and count but also watch out for the eighth-note rests.

Line 4

This line is a mixture of the previous three lines. Be sure to take your time and count consistently.

Line 5

We introduce 16th notes here. Count "1-e-&-ah" throughout the line. Counting 16th notes is tricky, as there is a lot to say, but it will help you identify mistakes and hear the differences in the note values. Nailing down these 16th notes is important because they're generally the smallest rhythmic value you'll encounter, making other values (quarters, eighths, etc.) easier to count and play.

Line 6

This 16th-note line incorporates eighth rests. Remember, an eighth rest has the same rhythmic value (i.e., half a beat) as an eighth note.

Line 7

This line uses eighth rests to break up the 16th-note groupings, which is very common. Just remember: two 16ths equal one eighth note.

Line 8

This line introduces the 16th rest, which allows us to pull one 16th note away from the others, giving us lots of combinations.

Line 9

More combinations of 16th notes and 16th rests.

Line 10

Here, we break up the notes with 16th rests and eighth rests. If you're not counting, this is where the music can get really confusing.

Line 11

In this next line, we connect eighth notes and 16th notes, using 16th rests to complete the remaining time. Remember that, when reading music, you must account for all notes and rests, and these values must add up to one complete measure—in this case, four beats, or, in smallest terms, sixteen 16th notes.

Line 12

This line combines much of what we've gone over in Lines 1–11.

Line 13

Here, we continue to combine 16th rests, 16th notes, and eighth notes.

Line 14

This line moves the 16th notes to the off-beats (the "e" and "ah"), which can be tricky to navigate.

Line 15

Our last portion of reading gets us into triplets, an integral part of most Western music. With triplets, the beat is divided into thirds. Therefore, we employ some different counting to keep time. Triplets use various note values, including quarter notes, eighth notes, and 16ths, but we label them with either a "3" or "6." In this book, we'll only use eighth-note triplets and 16th-note triplets, or sextuplets. The counting for eighth-note triplets is: "1-trip-let, 2-trip-let, 3-trip-let, 4-trip-let," with each syllable getting a snare strike (if there's a note).

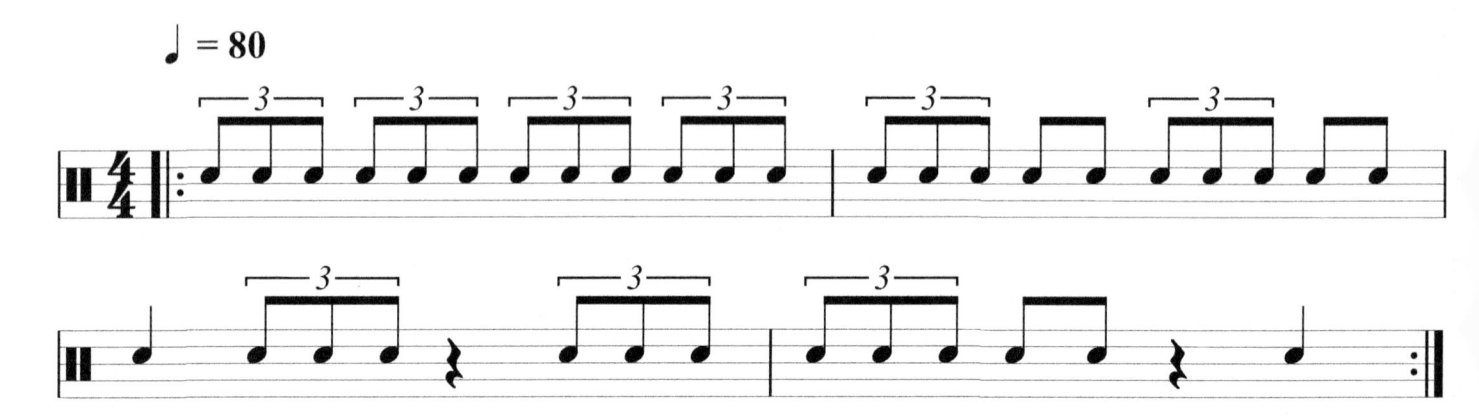

Line 16

Sixteenth-note triplets, or sextuplets, are pretty fast but don't feel the need to rush through them. With sextuplets, three 16th notes fit into the space of a single eighth note, which, when played across a single beat (two eighth notes), can be counted as: "1-trip-let-and-trip-let," etc. Alternately, when the music gets faster—and you're comfortable—you can just count "1-and, 2-and, 3-and, 4-and" while playing the notes in the appropriate spots.

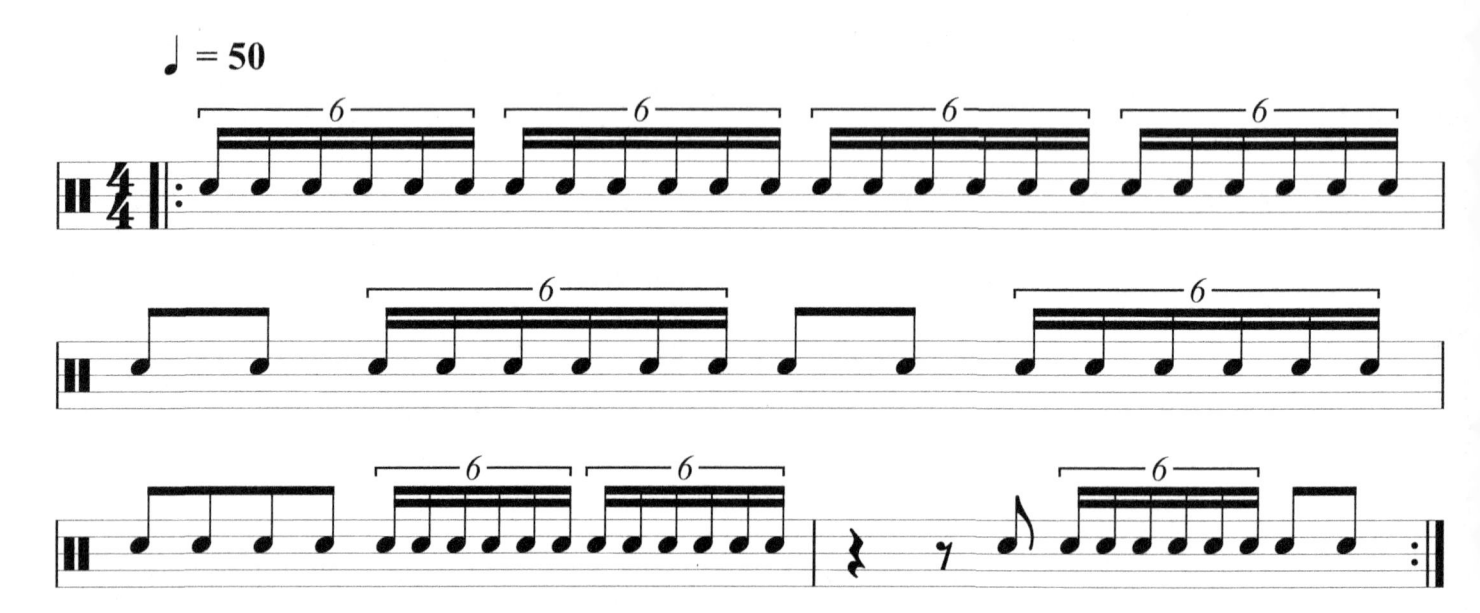

Line 17

This next line features combinations of 16th-note triplets, sextuplets, eighth notes, and eighth rests.

Line 18

Here, we introduce the "flam," which is a rudiment that is common in all forms of music. To perform the flam, strike the grace note just before the main note. Think of the flam as a way to "thicken" your sound.

Line 19

This line uses the flam on eighth notes.

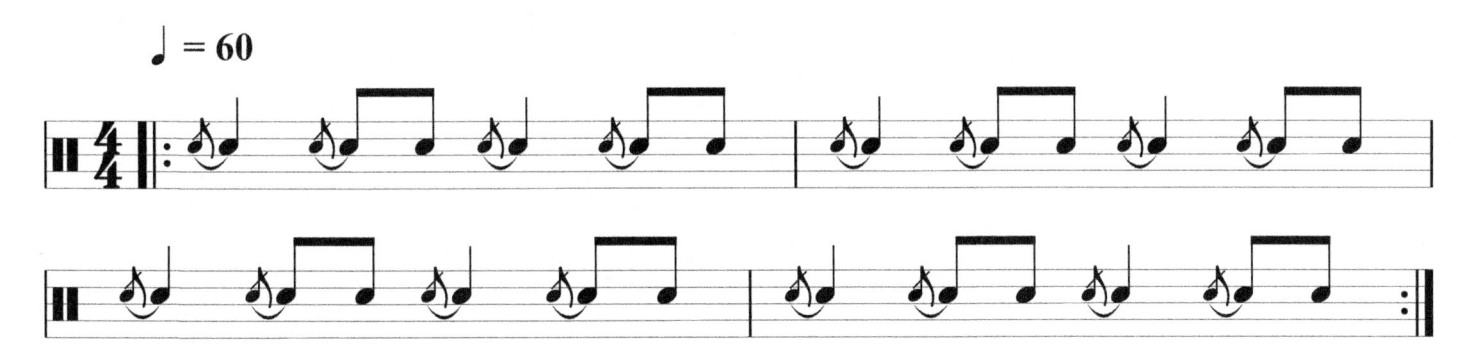

Line 20

Our final line uses the flam on 16th notes.

DAY 1

The first day of material has you working all four limbs. If you have a hard time assembling them all, then take one at a time or in pairs, gradually adding a limb as you go. Make sure you give yourself enough time to read and react—in other words, go slowly. A lot of what you'll initially be working on will be isolating the bass drum from the rest of the kit to develop some limb independence and the ability to sort through and learn grooves from songs.

In rock music, most often it's the bass drum that changes patterns from song to song by either adding or subtracting a note or two. Why? Because the bass drum rhythms need to fit the rhythmic structure of the song, as well as work with the part the bassist is playing. Usually, the snare stays pretty consistent (i.e., on beats 2 and 4) and the ride hand repeats an unchanging figure for most of the song. There are countless variables, of course, but we will start by taking things one step at time, increasing your independence gradually. Remember to play steadily and, once you've internalized a pattern, listen to your sound, focusing on making everything sound balanced.

Lastly, strive to play each pattern consistently for 30–60 seconds without stopping. This will prepare you for playing whole songs. Use and trust your ears to guide how you strike the instrument. Try not to tense your grip or play *into* the surfaces; instead, you want the sticks and pedals to spring off of what you hit, getting you ready to make the next strike. If you let the drum resonate freely, your natural sound will develop!

PATTERN 1 (1:30–1:15)

Our first pattern incorporates all four limbs. It's important to get all the limbs working so that nothing sits unused. The biggest challenge is always the weak side, so we'll get that working by closing the hi-hat with the snare on beats 2 and 4.

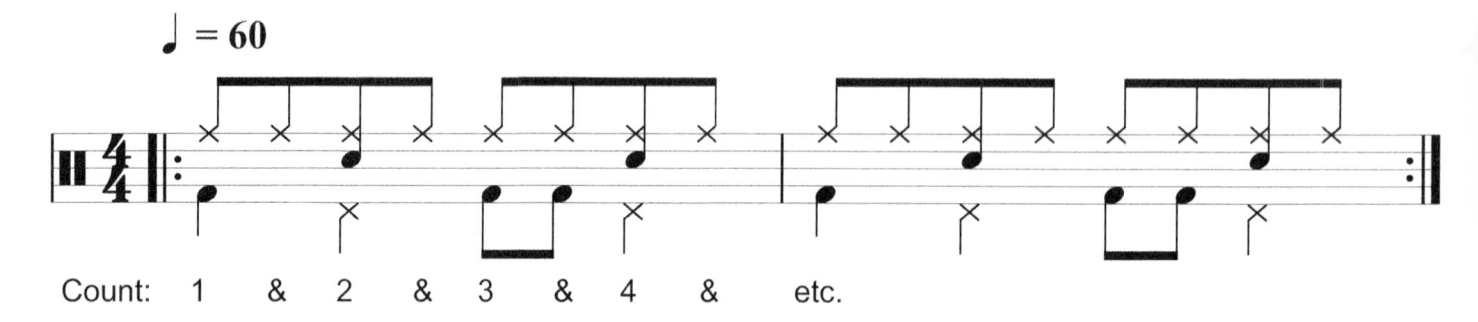

PATTERN 2 (1:15–1:00)

Pattern 2 is the same as Pattern 1 but now you play the hi-hat closed. Play the hi-hat with the hand that feels best to you, whether you cross over the top with your dominant hand or open with your other hand (uncrossed).

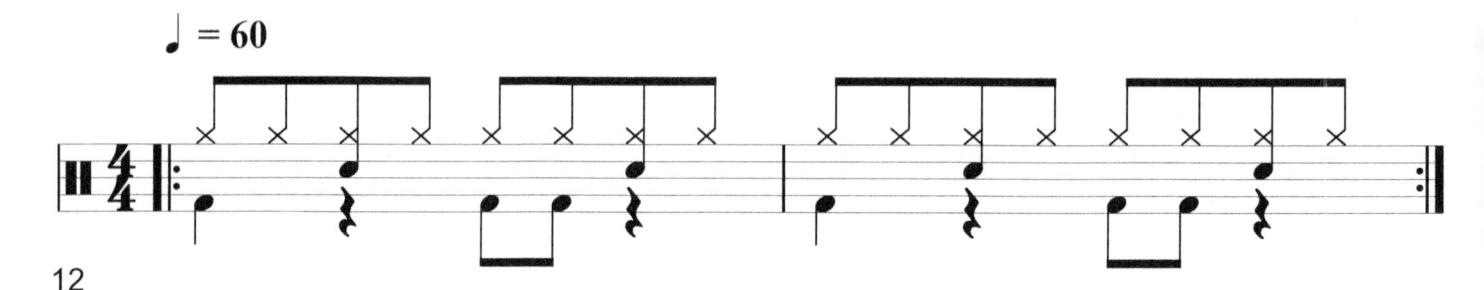

PATTERN 3 (1:00–0:45)

Here, we use eighth rests to allow us to place bass drum notes on the "and" of beats 2 and 4 and go back to riding on the cymbal and closing the hi-hat with the foot (the foot hi-hats are notated in place of the bass drum eighth rests for ease of reading).

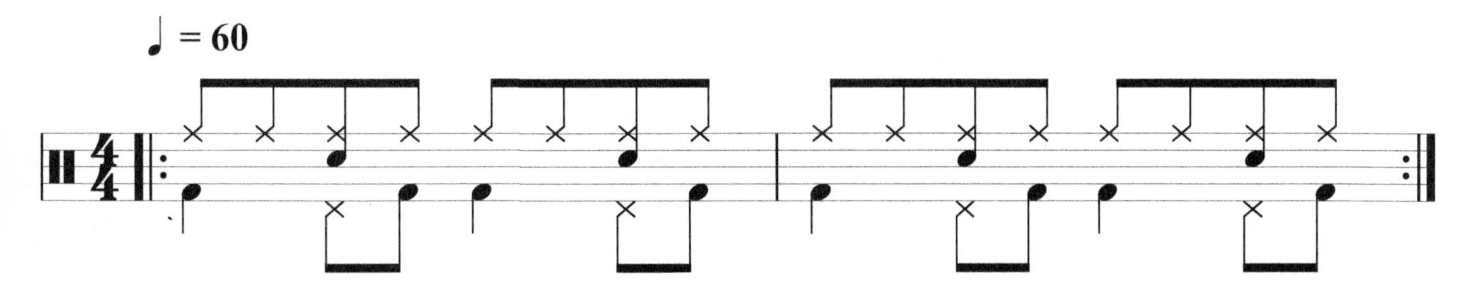

PATTERN 4 (0:45–0:30)

Pattern 4 uses an eighth rest to remove a note from beat 3 of each measure, which may feel odd to you at first. Make sure your counting is steady and continues through the whole measure.

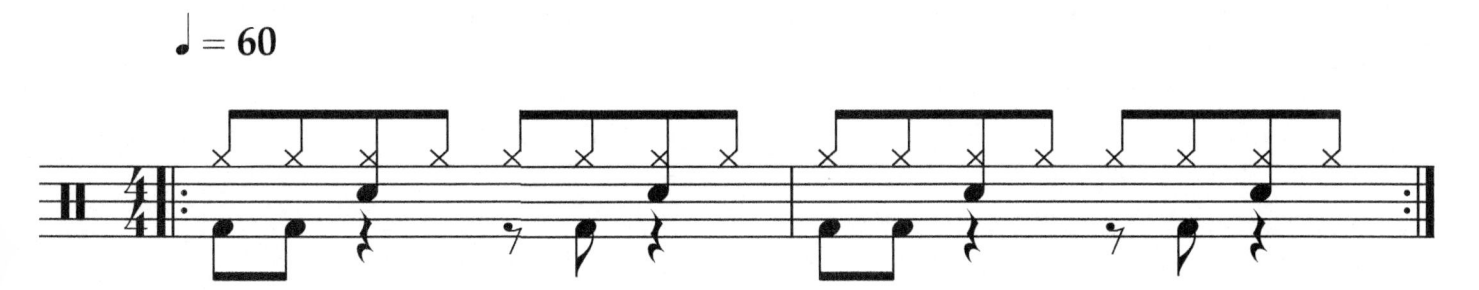

PATTERN 5 (0:30–0:15)

Pattern 5 introduces the quarter-note ride cymbal pattern, which will be your first step in playing the bass drum in a spot where no ride note is happening. This might present a challenge, as your hand and foot may want to follow one another, so go slow enough to control each limb. By doing so, you'll begin to develop your limb independence!

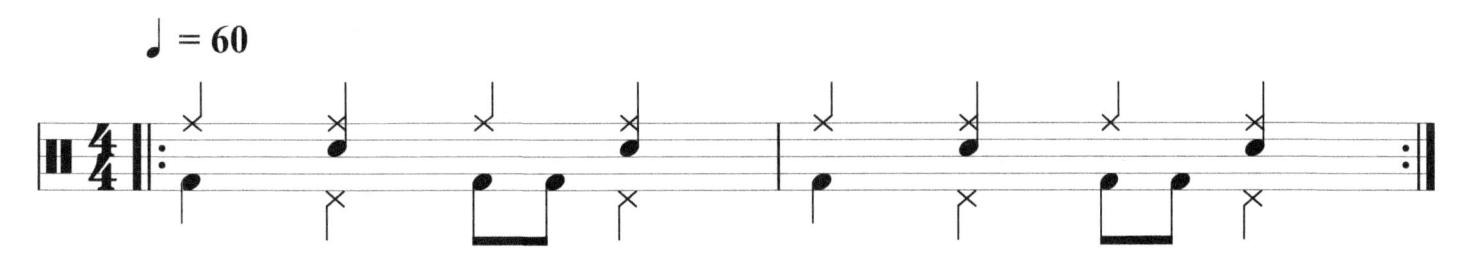

PATTERN 6 (0:15–0:00)

We wrap up Day 1 with some quarter note ride patterns and move the bass drum to the end of beats 2 and 4. It might feel odd to have all that space between bass drum hits but you'll get used to it.

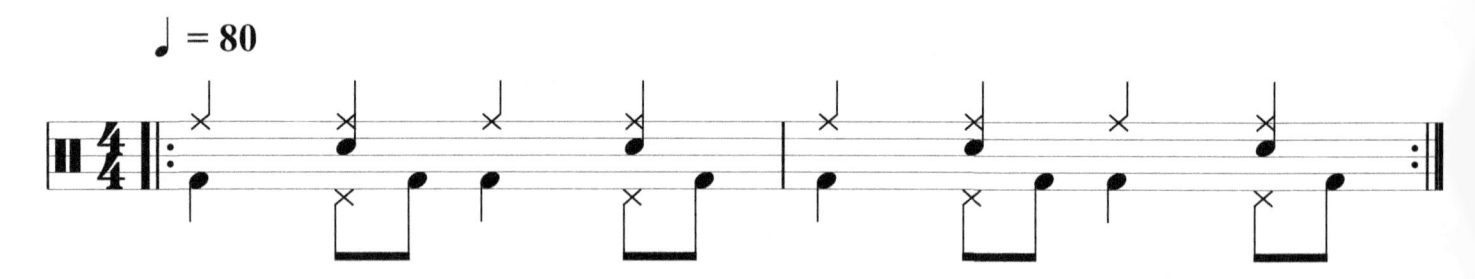

Congrats! You made it through Day 1! Take a bit of time either now or another day to listen to some of the suggested songs listed below and research some of the drummers I have included. Study the trailblazers, as it will help you to build a solid foundation and appreciation of what has come before you and how this instrument has evolved.

SUGGESTED LISTENING
- "Free Fallin'" Tom Petty & the Heartbreakers
- "Another One Bites the Dust" Queen
- "Billie Jean" Michael Jackson
- "Pretty Please" Dua Lipa
- "Sgt. Pepper's Lonely Hearts Club Band" The Beatles

FIVE DRUMMERS TO STUDY
- Earl Palmer
- Hal Blaine
- Ringo Starr
- Charlie Watts
- Gary Chester

DAY 2

Today's lesson contains a bit less content as we shift our focus to some new elements.

PATTERN 1 (1:30–1:10)

We start by continuing to work the bass drum against a quarter-note ride pattern.

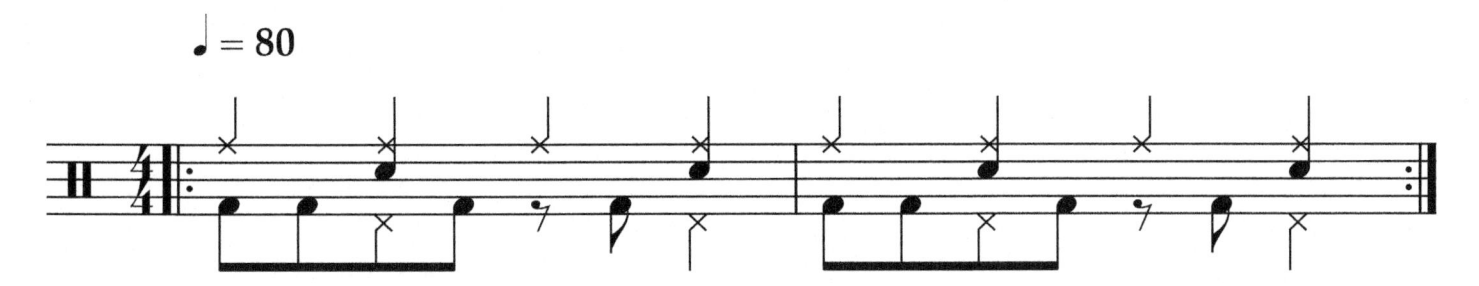

PATTERN 2 (1:10–0:50)

This pattern is tricky because it's the first time you won't be playing the bass drum on beat 1. This pattern will feel odd at first but it's common to play two-measure patterns that feature a rest on beat 1.

PATTERN 3 (0:50–0:30)

Pattern 3 is your introduction to drum fills. A *drum fill* can be any deviation from the static pattern you're playing, with a return back to said pattern. As long as it serves the song, a fill can be complex, simple, lots of notes, or hardly any notes at all. The time frame can vary, too, but for now, we'll limit the fills to one measure, which will help you to internalize measure length so you can work freely and creatively within that time span.

The first fill (measure 2) is a string of 16th notes to be played on the snare before returning to the beat (measure 1). Once you feel comfortable, try moving your hands to another surface of your choice (listen to the audio to hear two variations), focusing on the balance of sound as you complete the pattern. Try any combinations that you can think of but take your time and remember to play as steady as possible and without rushing. Otherwise, your fill will likely sound unbalanced and out of time. Your biggest challenge will be moving from surface to surface, so make sure you give yourself the time to develop those moves, and gradually you'll get comfortable.

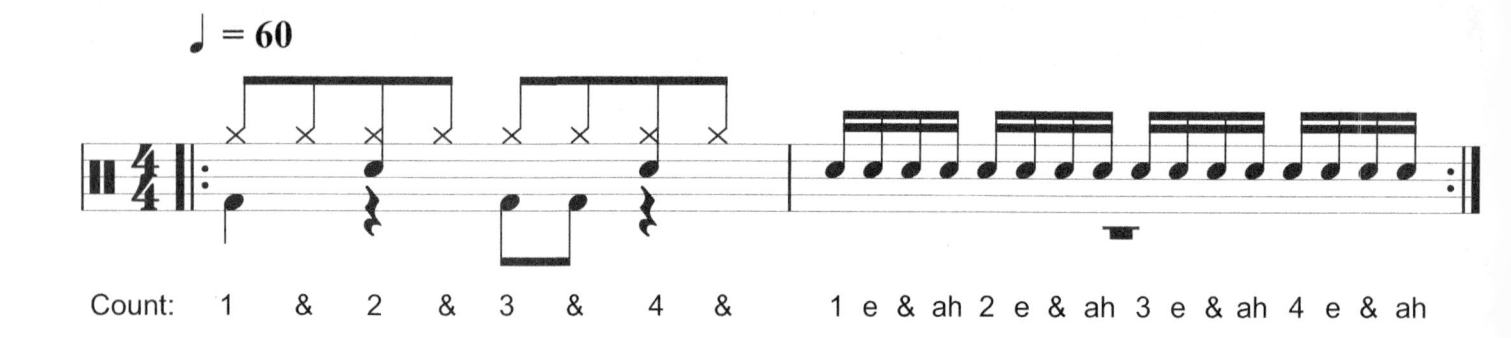

Count: 1 & 2 & 3 & 4 &   1 e & ah 2 e & ah 3 e & ah 4 e & ah

PATTERN 4 (0:30–0:00)

For this beat, we switch to a quarter-note ride pattern and bring the hi-hat back with the foot. You can try different sticking combinations if you like but I suggest starting with alternate strokes, leading with your dominant hand. The audio features a couple of variations, all of which are performed with alternate sticking (RLRL), to give you some ideas on how to move around the kit.

SUGGESTED LISTENING	FIVE DRUMMERS TO STUDY
• "Vertigo" U2	• Levon Helm
• "All Right Now" Free	• Jim Gordon
• "Problem Child" AC/DC	• Jeff Porcaro
• "Jumpin' Jack Flash" The Rolling Stones	• Ginger Baker
• "Starlight" Muse	• Keith Moon

DAY 3

If you've progressed through 16th notes in the Basic Music Reading section, then you're ready to tackle the material on Day 3. This is where we start to incorporate different groupings of 16th notes into the bass drum patterns. Take your time placing the notes in the correct spots, making sure to count "1-e-&-ah" through every measure, regardless if you're playing 16th notes at the time or not. That approach will help you to hear and understand the different rhythmic subdivisions and how they relate to one another. It will also help you place the notes in the correct spots and keep your limbs from jumping when you add the notes to the mix.

PATTERN 1 (1:30–1:10)

Our first pattern places a 16th note on the "e" of beats 1 and 3.

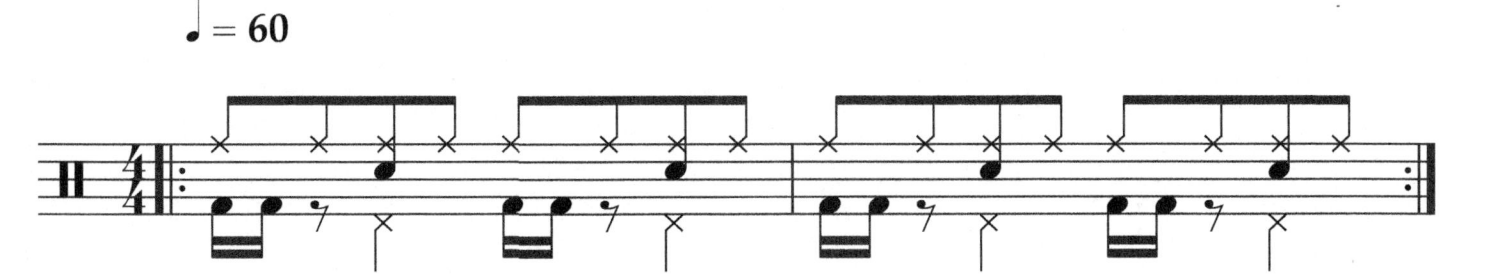

PATTERN 2 (1:10–0:50)

Pattern 2 is the same as Pattern 1 but your ride hand is now on the hi-hat.

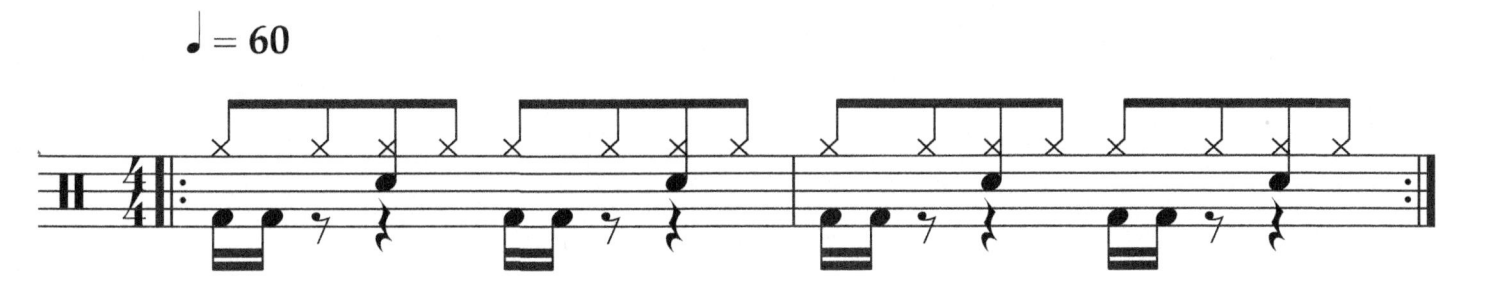

PATTERN 3 (0:50–0:30)

Now we return to playing a drum fill. Apply the same idea as before: moving your hands about the kit once you get comfortable playing the sequence of notes on the snare.

PATTERN 4 (0:30–0:00)

Here's another fill combination. This time, the beat has you returning your ride hand to the cymbal and closing the hi-hat on beats 2 and 4. Again, spend a good amount of time exploring the kit with the fill, enjoying finding new combinations of sounds while breaking up the notes between the drums and cymbals.

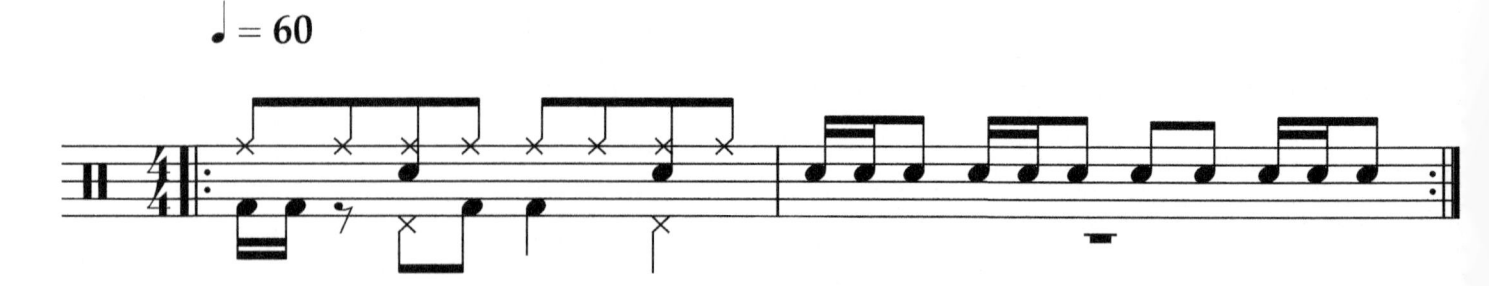

SUGGESTED LISTENING	FIVE DRUMMERS TO STUDY
• "Lucille" Little Richard	• Steve Jordan
• "Sad but True" Metallica	• Mitch Mitchell
• "Yummy" Justin Bieber	• John Bonham
• "Green Onions" Booker T & the MGs	• Bill Ward
• "Vultures" John Mayer	• Steve Gadd

DAY 4

Today, we further explore 16th-note patterns and fill combinations.

PATTERN 1 (1:30–1:15)

Here's a groove featuring 16th notes and eighth notes.

PATTERN 2 (1:15–1:00)

The drum fill (measure 1) contains 16th notes, eighth notes, and eighth rests. Make sure to count so you get the spacing of the notes correct. After the fill, we add a crash on beat 1 (measure 2). To make the sound, you can hit your ride cymbal with the neck of your stick or strike another cymbal. We will do more "crashing" later on, too!

PATTERN 3 (1:00–0:45)

Measure 2 features another fill but this time the hi-hat is held partially open for the beat. This is common for rock beats. Just relax your foot a little bit, and the cymbals should open slightly. Strike the hi-hat moderately—but not too hard—and it should make a nice, splashy sound.

PATTERN 4 (0:45–0:30)

Now we slide back over to the ride cymbal and close the hi-hat on beats 2 and 4 while adding a new 16th-note bass drum pattern.

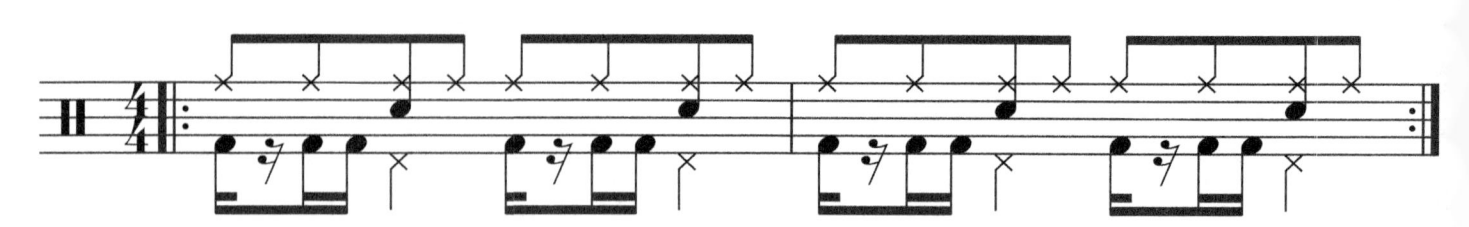

PATTERN 5 (0:30–0:15)

Pattern 5 takes us back to the partially opened hi-hat, this time playing eighth notes, as well as playing some bass drum hits on the "ands" of beats 2 and 4.

PATTERN 6 (0:15–0:00)

A three-note grouping on the bass drum is happening in this pattern. It might be a challenge to lock those notes down consistently, so, again, make sure you're going slow enough to play each note cleanly and without strain. Over time, this will get smoother and easier.

SUGGESTED LISTENING	FIVE DRUMMERS TO STUDY
• "Immigrant Song" Led Zeppelin	• Questlove
• "Iron Man" Black Sabbath	• Kenny Aronoff
• "I Can't Explain" The Who	• Cindy Blackman Santana
• "Moves Like Jagger" Marron 5	• Sheila E.
• "Uptown Funk" Mark Ronson	• Roger Hawkins

DAY 5

We are really into the thick of the book now, with a solid emphasis on integrating 16ths with eighth notes and various rests, as well as mixing up the different ways to approach your ride hand.

PATTERN 1 (1:30–1:15)

This pattern leads off with a fill based on a motif of three 16th notes, which reappears in the beat pattern (see the bass drum).

PATTERN 2 (1:15–1:00)

Things get a bit trickier in Pattern 2, as we combine different three-note groupings of 16ths with eighth notes. Lots to play here!

PATTERN 3 (1:00–0:45)

This pattern brings back the partially open hi-hat and features more note combinations for the fill. There's also a crash on beat 1 of the beat (measure 2). It may be tricky to hit the crash and then move to the hi-hat, so go slowly at first.

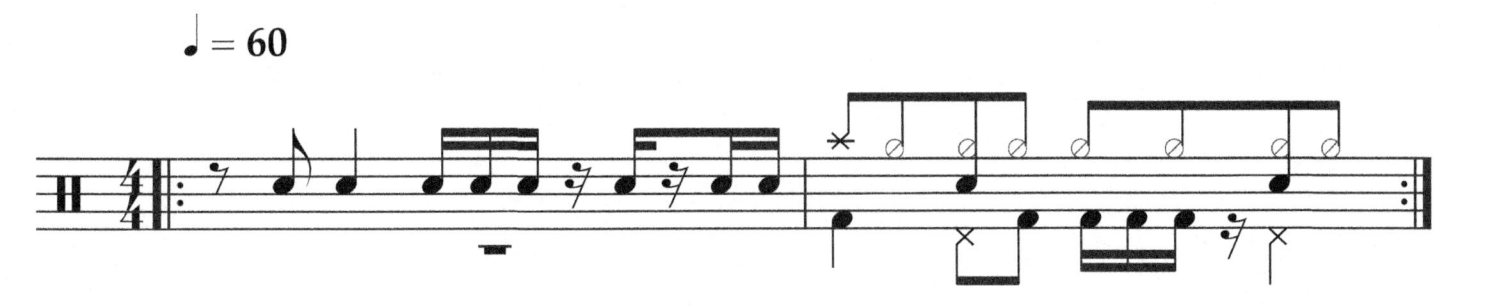

PATTERN 4 (0:45–0:30)

This pattern incorporates the flam, which is used to play a classic fill that alternates eighth notes between the snare and bass drum. You can move the flam to the toms, as well, or any other surface of the kit!

PATTERN 5 (0:30–0:15)

Pattern 5 may look easy but the rests on beat 1 of each measure can be tricky. Make sure to count and enjoy how this note combination makes the fill a bit more interesting.

PATTERN 6 (0:15–0:00)

Today's final pattern brings in a common note grouping that features notes on the beat (the number) and on the "ah" of the same beat. This usually isn't too difficult; just make sure your lead hand doesn't jump.

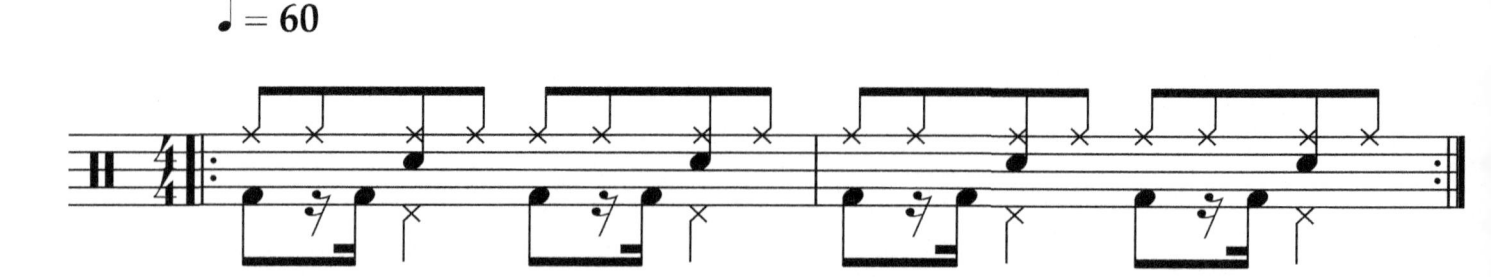

SUGGESTED LISTENING	FIVE DRUMMERS TO STUDY
• "Imagine" John Lennon	• Jim Keltner
• "Up on Cripple Creek" The Band	• Josh Freese
• "Dreams" Fleetwood Mac	• Matt Cameron
• "Respect" Aretha Franklin	• Bernard Purdie
• "The Ghost of You" My Chemical Romance	• Ian Paice

DAY 6

Today, we continue onward with more combinations of 16th and eighth notes, as well as more fill ideas.

PATTERN 1 (1:30–1:15)

This pattern uses an eighth note with a 16th on the "ah" for a fill. There is a lot of space to account for, making this fill tricky to learn at first.

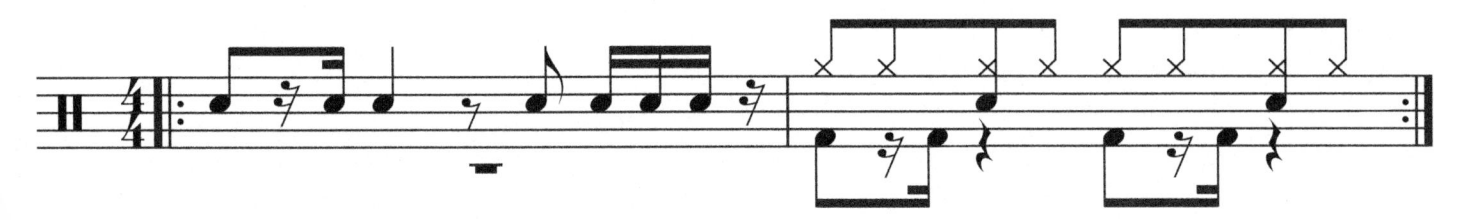

PATTERN 2 (1:15–1:00)

This mixed beat pattern brings back the foot hi-hats on beats 2 and 4.

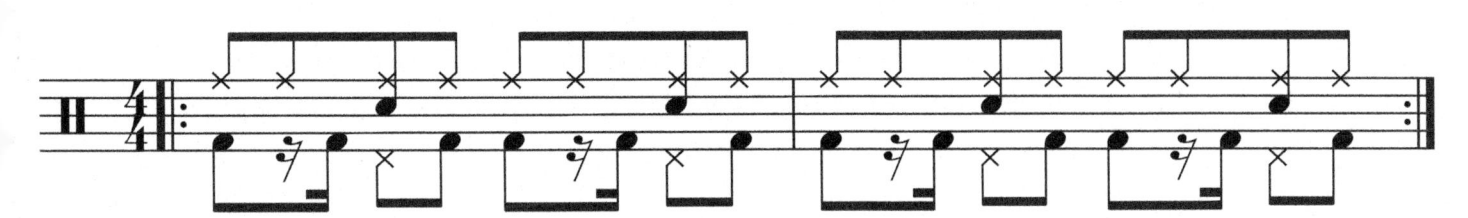

PATTERN 3 (1:00–0:45)

Here, we switch the ride hand to partially opened hi-hats.

PATTERN 4 (0:45–0:30)

Pattern 4 introduces a new three-note pattern in the bass drum. Be sure to count!

♩ = 60

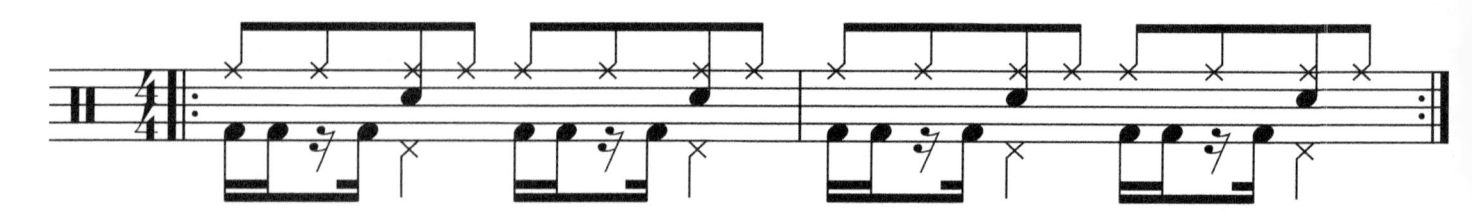

PATTERN 5 (0:30–0:15)

Now we take the three-note combination from Pattern 4 and apply it to a fill idea.

♩ = 60

PATTERN 6 (0:15–0:00)

Here's a fill/beat combo that uses elements that you've learned today. An added twist is the crash on beat 1. It's a bit tricky due to the bass drum landing on the "e" immediately afterwards, so take it slow.

♩ = 60

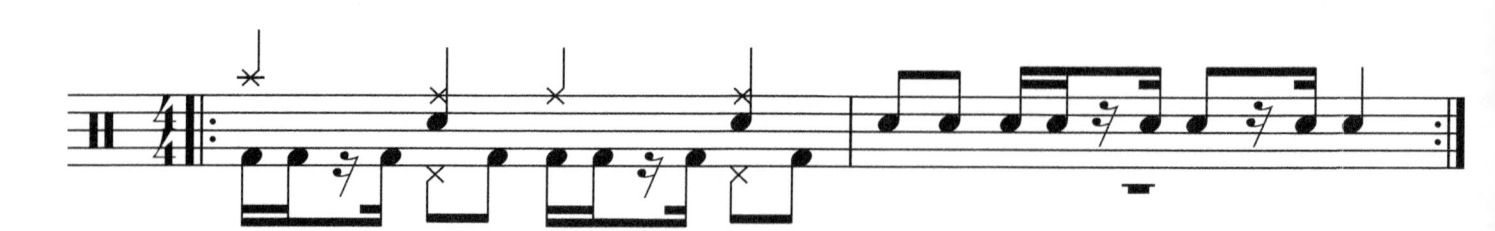

SUGGESTED LISTENING
- "You Belong to Me" Carly Simon
- "Back on the Chain Gang" Pretenders
- "My Boyfriend's Back" The Angels
- "Another Brick in the Wall" Pink Floyd
- "Heart of Gold" Neil Young

FIVE DRUMMERS TO STUDY
- Larry Mullen Jr.
- Carmine Appice
- Moe Tucker
- Ash Soan
- Larrie Londin

DAY 7

Now we change things up a bit in our ride hand, going to a two-handed, 16th-note hi-hat pattern. You can use any sticking pattern that you like but usually this hi-hat pattern is performed with an alternating sequence (for example, RLRL), which is briefly interrupted to strike the snare on beats 2 and 4.

We take a break from fills today but feel free to review any of the ones from a previous day to keep things fresh.

PATTERN 1 (1:30–1:15)
We add bass drum on every beat, which gives this groove an EDM-type feel.

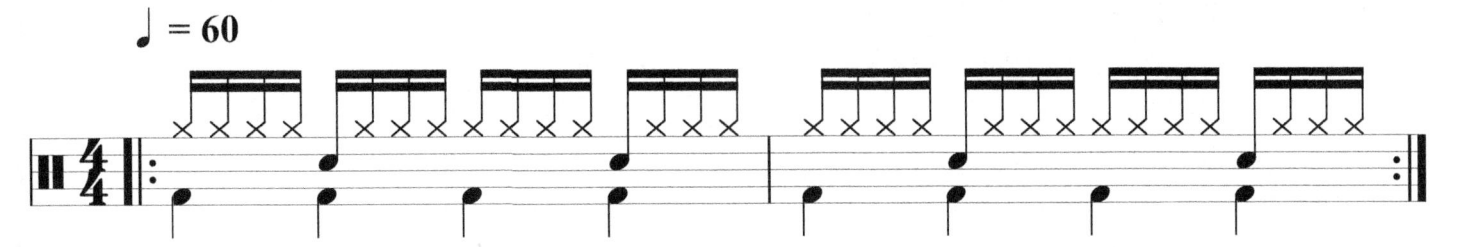

PATTERN 2 (1:15–1:00)
We apply eighth notes to the groove here. Be sure to count to get the hands and foot lined up correctly.

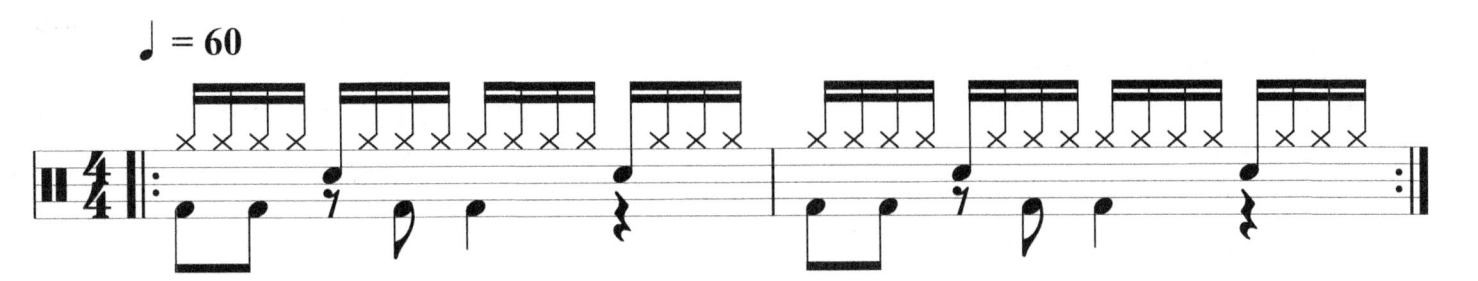

PATTERN 3 (1:00–0:45)
Here, 16th notes are added to the bass drum, which might trip you up a bit.

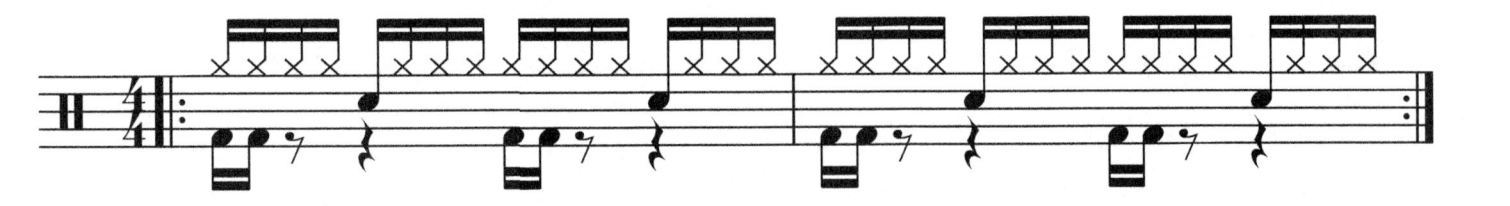

PATTERN 4 (0:45–0:30)

A mixture of eighth notes, 16th notes, and rests comprise this groove.

♩ = 60

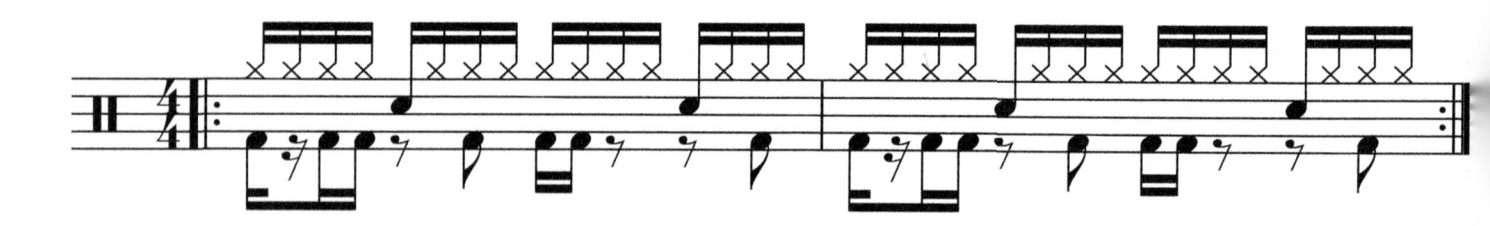

PATTERN 5 (0:30–0:15)

This pattern incorporates note groupings from the previous week.

♩ = 60

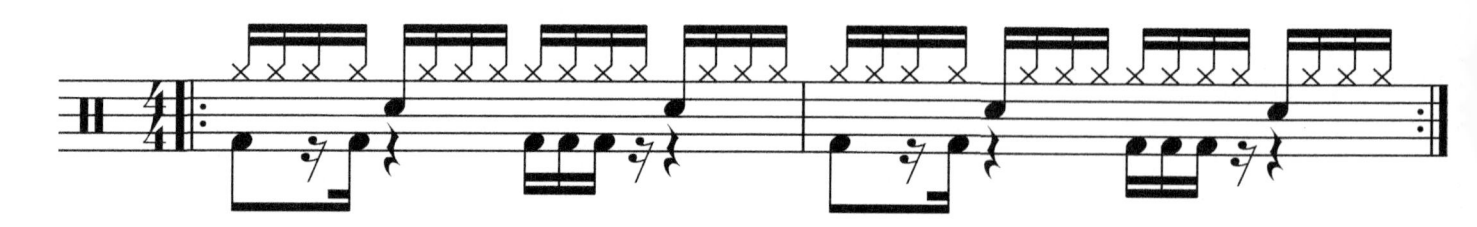

PATTERN 6 (0:15–0:00)

We wrap up today's work with a new twist: a complete two-measure beat whose second measure is different from the first. It's really common to hear this in all forms of music, even being applied to four-measure phrases, and we'll be seeing more of this later in the book.

♩ = 60

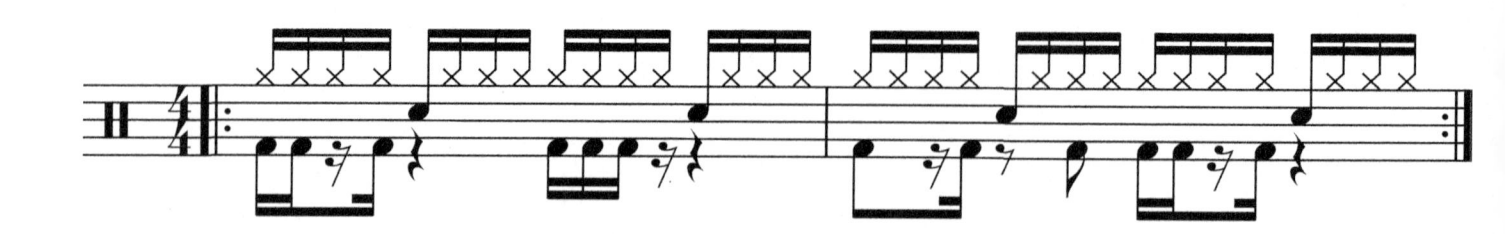

SUGGESTED LISTENING	FIVE DRUMMERS TO STUDY
• "Smoke on the Water" Deep Purple	• Phil Rudd
• "Oh! Sweet Nuthin'" The Velvet Underground	• Chad Smith
• "Kiss" Prince	• Cozy Powell
• "Spit of You" Sam Fender	• Phil Collins
• "Highway Tune" Greta Van Fleet	• Hannah Welton

DAY 8

Today, we begin to work on triplets. Triplets are an integral part of rock music… all forms of music, really. You'll often find grooves that use triplets as their foundation, and often the drummer will play fills solely based on them. Triplets don't have to be the foundation of the groove, however. Sometimes only parts of triplets are used, or triplets are combined with other note types.

Before you get started, be sure that you're comfortable with the triplet exercises in the Basic Music Reading section in front of the book, as they will prepare you for what is coming next. Also, listening to the audio examples will let you hear how triplets work with the other notes you've been working on up to this point. Be patient! Some of this may be a bit difficult at first.

PATTERN 1 (1:30–1:15)

This pattern uses triplets for a fill (measure 1) and places an accent on the first note of every set of 3. To play an accent, keep the other notes quieter and strike the accented note a bit louder. The beat you're playing after the fill (measure 2) is reminiscent of a classic blues beat but it's a good starting point for learning triplet-oriented beat patterns. We'll expand on this groove later.

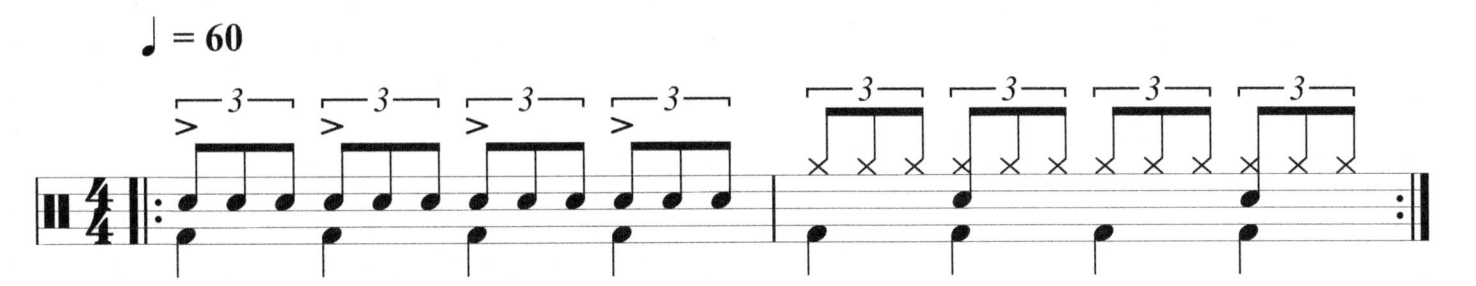

PATTERN 2 (1:15–1:00)

This next groove breaks up the bass drum pattern in measure 1, which is followed by a fill consisting of straight triplets. Feel free to expand the fill by moving your hands about the kit. You'll notice that your leading hand ends up in different spots due to the odd note groupings. Consequently, you'll need to work on developing the control to play evenly and cleanly.

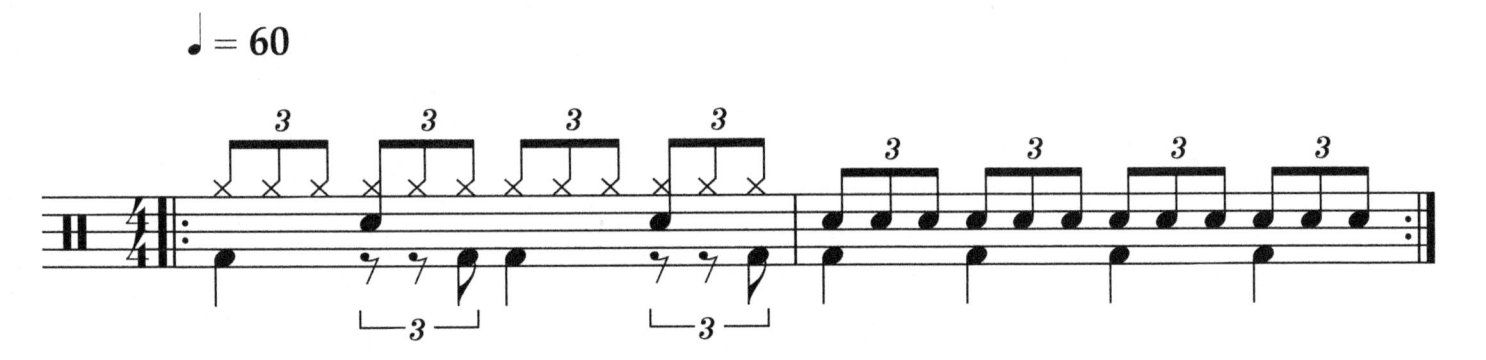

PATTERN 3 (1:00–0:45)

We break away from a triplet-oriented beat pattern and switch to a quarter-note ride (measure 2). This is very common in rock and other styles of music. You'll use triplets very frequently, not just in triplet-oriented grooves, so it's important that you're able hear and play them in "straight time." The tempo is sped up here (90 BPM) so you can play the quarter notes more comfortably but if you need to play it slower, then by all means do it to develop confidence and control.

PATTERN 4 (0:45–0:30)

Now we switch to partially opened, eighth-note hi-hats, along with the familiar triplet fill.

PATTERN 5 (0:30–0:15)

The triplet fill (measure 1) gets broken up by eighth notes here and we apply 16th notes to the bass drum in the beat pattern. Again, feel free to slide around the kit and experiment with the new notes when playing the fill.

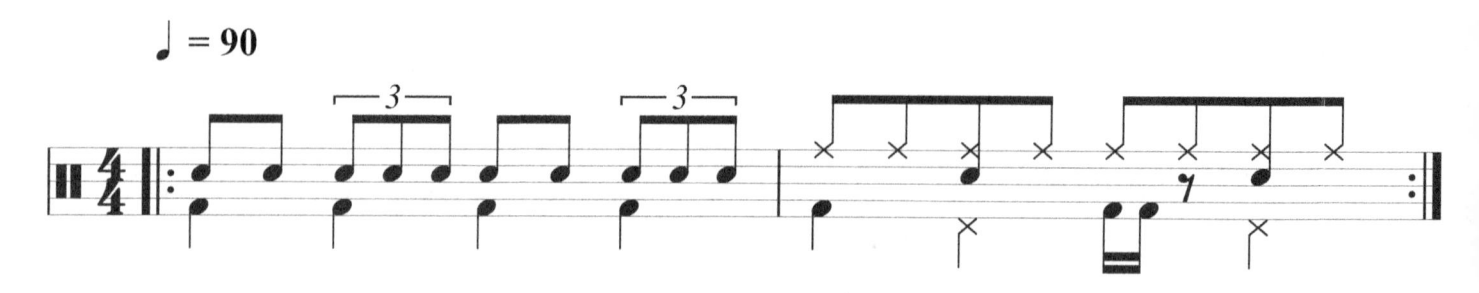

PATTERN 6 (0:15–0:00)

Pattern 6 is a bit trickier due to the addition of 16th notes in the fill (measure 2). We slow the tempo back down a bit here (70 BPM) but, if you feel up to it, you can push it upward. Be sure to listen to the audio, as it might be hard to count and feel the varying note values.

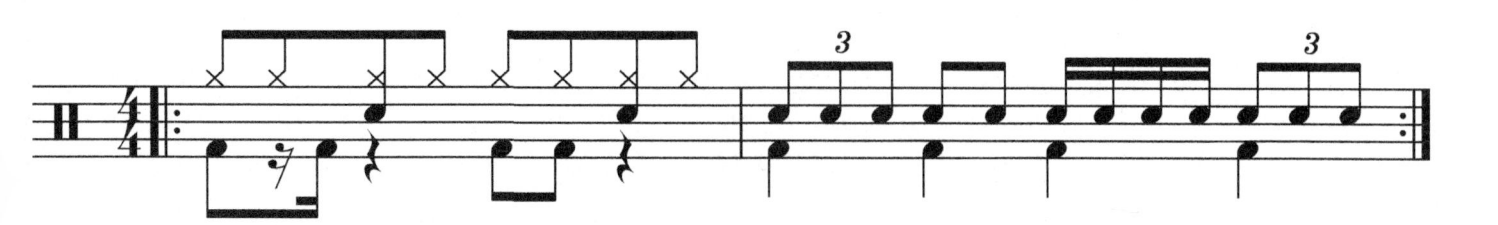

SUGGESTED LISTENING
- "And the Cradle Will Rock" Van Halen
- "Up on Cripple Creek" The Band
- "Pressure and Time" Rival Sons
- "If I Ever Lose My Faith in You" Sting
- "Tales of Brave Ulysses" Cream

FIVE DRUMMERS TO STUDY
- Karen Carpenter
- Stewart Copeland
- Joey Kramer
- Dennis Chambers
- Phil Selway

DAY 9

Today, we'll continue to incorporate triplet figures into the work, focusing on 16th-note triplets, or "sextuplets." Sixteenth-note triplets are twice as fast as eighth-note triplets, so you'll need to fight the urge to rush them. We also introduce a few 16th-note combinations that you have yet to encounter. None of it is too difficult if you maintain your counting and take your time. Remember to play what you're reading and hearing, not what "think" it should be.

PATTERN 1 (1:30–1:15)

This string of 16th-note triplets (sextuplets) may be a bit daunting at first, so pull the tempo back and listen to the audio. The biggest problem drummers have with this type of figure is that the fill (measure 1) is not aligned with the tempo and, as a result, they start the beat (measure 2) too early.

Start with the fill and count. You can count two ways: "1-trip-let-and-trip-let, 2-trip-let-and-trip-let," etc. Or subdivide the beat into eighth notes and just count "1-and, 2-and, 3-and, 4-and," playing accents on each count (the numbers). The latter is the best way to count when the tempo is faster and for counting varying note values like the ones here.

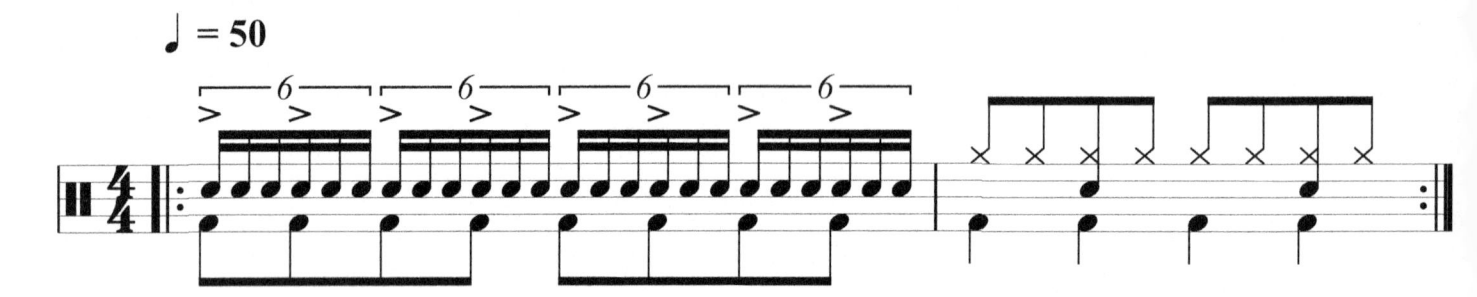

PATTERN 2 (1:15–1:00)

This pattern uses eighth rests to allow us to place 16th notes on the "and" and "ah" of beats 3 and 4 in measure 1, and beats 2 and 4 in measure 2.

PATTERN 3 (1:00–0:45)

In this example, we use the 16th rest to allow us to place bass drum notes on the "e" and "and" of beats 2 and 4 in measure 1, and beat 3 in measure 2, which will sort of feel like Pattern 2 but the notes land a bit quicker.

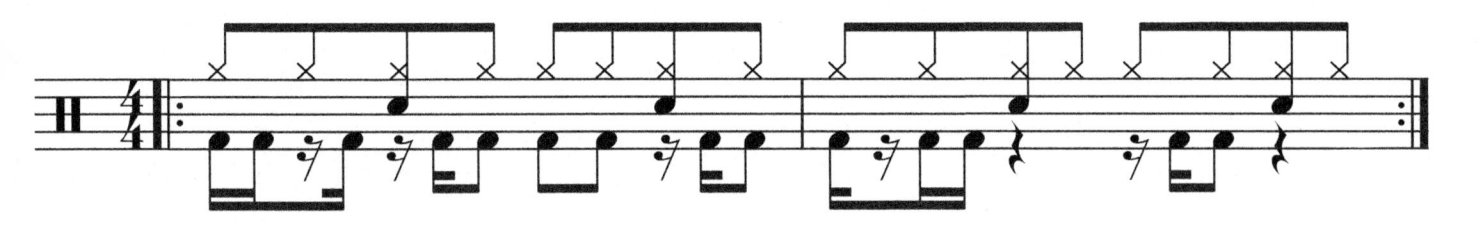

PATTERN 4 (0:45–0:30)

Here's another two-note change-up. This time, two 16th rests result in the notes landing on the "e" and "ah" (beat 3 in measure 1, beat 2 in measure 2).

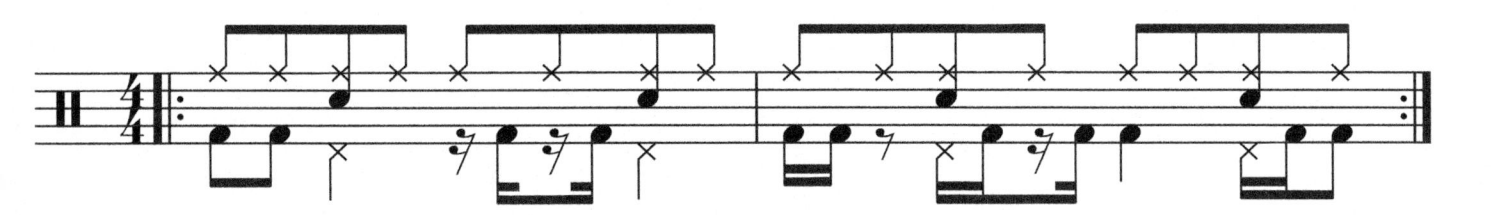

PATTERN 5 (0:30–0:15)

Pattern 5 adds a broken sextuplet to a fill idea, with an eighth note falling on the "and" of each beat. Remember, 16th-note triplets are faster than regular 16th notes, so don't count these four-note groupings "1-e-&-ah, 2-e-&-ah," etc. Instead, they should be counted "1-trip-let-and, 2-trip-let-and," etc. Listen to the audio for help.

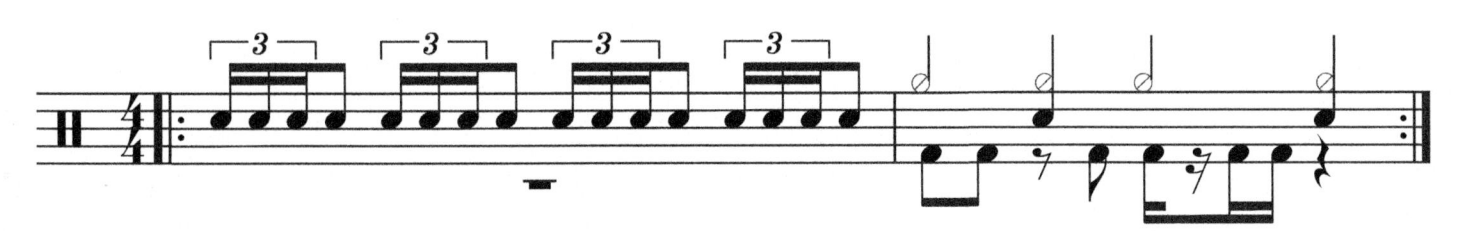

PATTERN 6 (0:15–0:00)

This pattern mixes the note values so you can see how 16th-note triplets and regular 16th notes sound in the same measure. The audio example will help you hear this. Move the fill notes (measure 2) around the kit when you're ready!

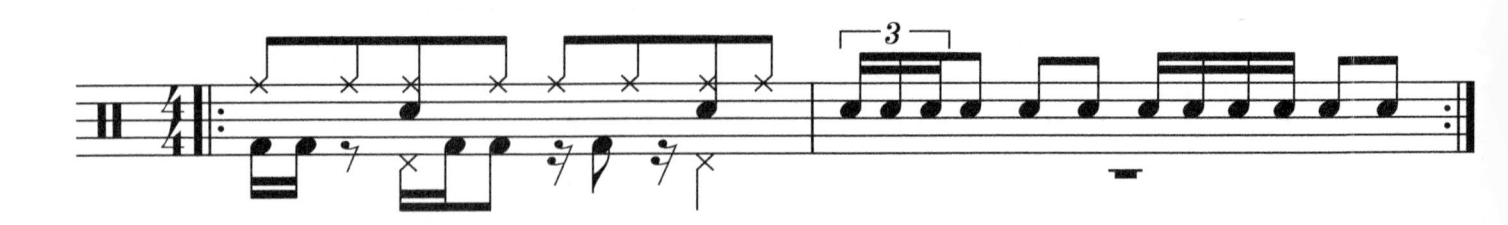

SUGGESTED LISTENING
- "All These Things That I've Done" The Killers
- "Bodysnatchers" Radiohead
- "Vacation" Devin Townsend
- "Lust for Life" Iggy Pop
- "The Momur" Adrian Belew

FIVE DRUMMERS TO STUDY
- Eddie Bayers
- Carter Beauford
- Richie Hayward
- Simon Phillips
- Vinnie Colaiuta

DAY 10

Day 10 gets us into a few new elements, including linear drum fills and 16th-note combinations, which involve freeing up the snare hand a little bit and working against the ride hand.

PATTERN 1 (1:30–1:15)

This pattern is a triplet-based groove often used in blues, as well as many other styles.

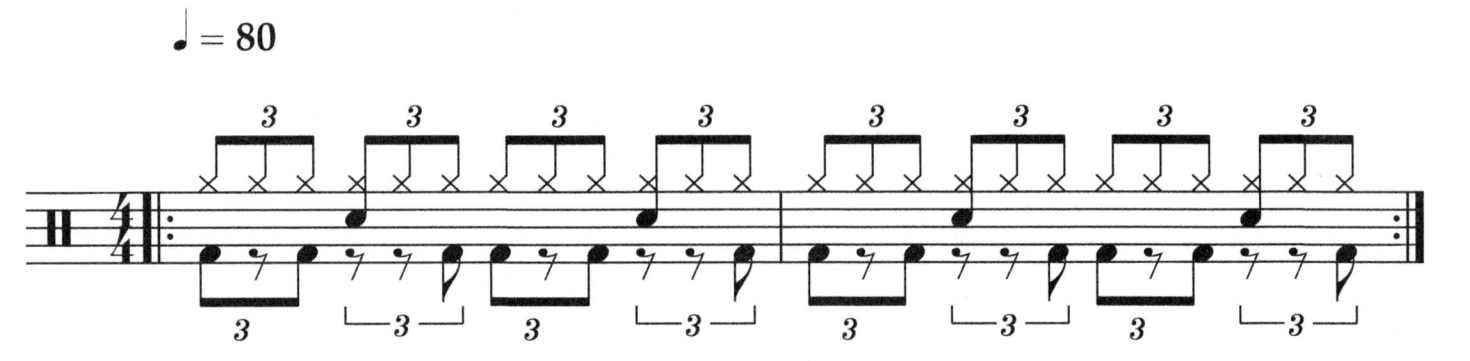

PATTERN 2 (1:15–1:00)

In our first linear fill (measure 2), triplets are broken up between the snare and bass drum. When you get this together, move your hands about the kit and work on blending the different surfaces with the bass drum. Watch the balance, however, so that the bass doesn't overpower your hands.

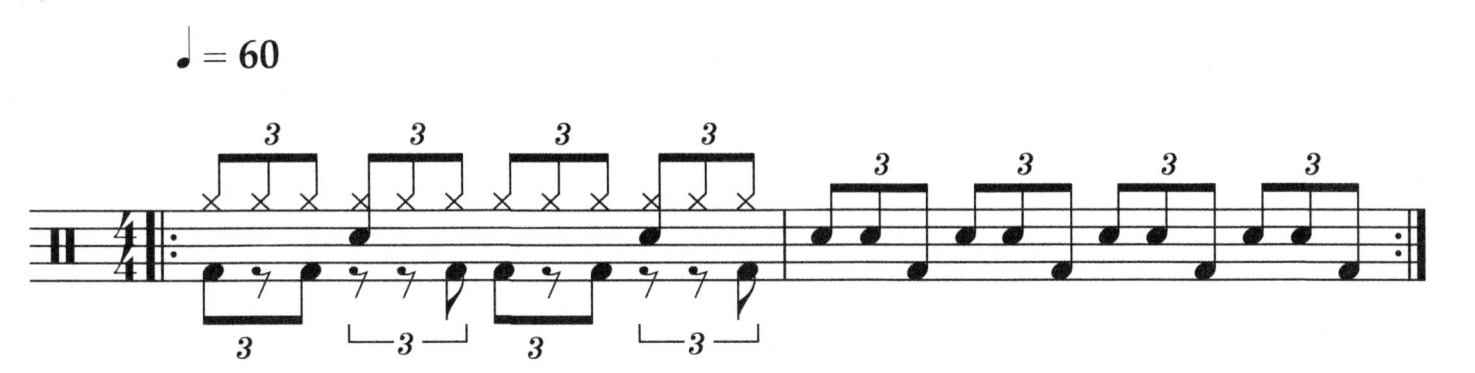

PATTERN 3 (1:00–0:45)

The pattern here works the snare in greater detail against your ride hand. The challenge will be to keep everything in line, so take your time.

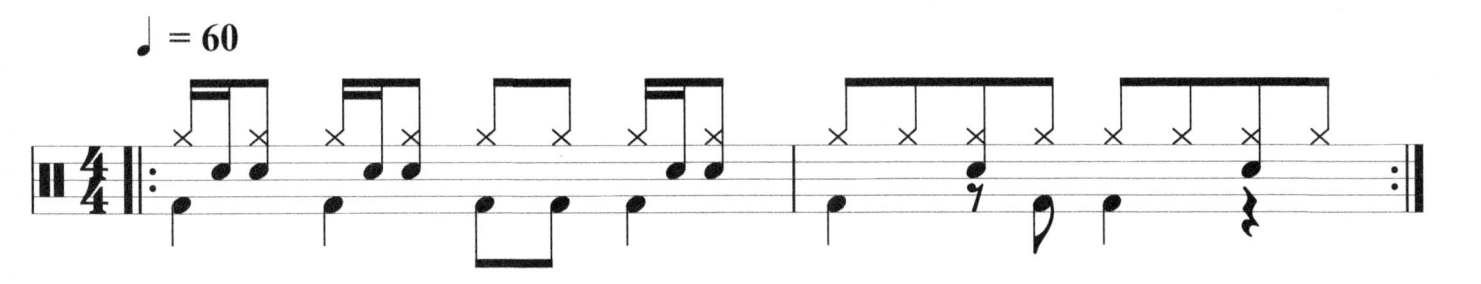

PATTERN 4 (0:45–0:30)

In this pattern, we shift the snare notes from Pattern 3 so they arrive one 16th note early in the measure.

PATTERN 5 (0:30–0:15)

Now we deal with a snare hit on the "e" of beats 1 and 3. Go slow enough so that your ride hand (on the hi-hat) holds steady.

PATTERNS 6A–B (0:15–0:00)

These patterns feature a popular set of linear fills using the bass drum and hands. You'll be seeing more combinations like these as we move through the book. These patterns can be looked at as both fill ideas and as exercises to build up foot speed and control (i.e., using your foot in combination with your hands). You could practice these linear fills in high repetitions, pushing the tempo up only as the notes become clean and even. If you work on them in a consistent manner, you can build up some nice speed, control, and power.

Pattern 6A

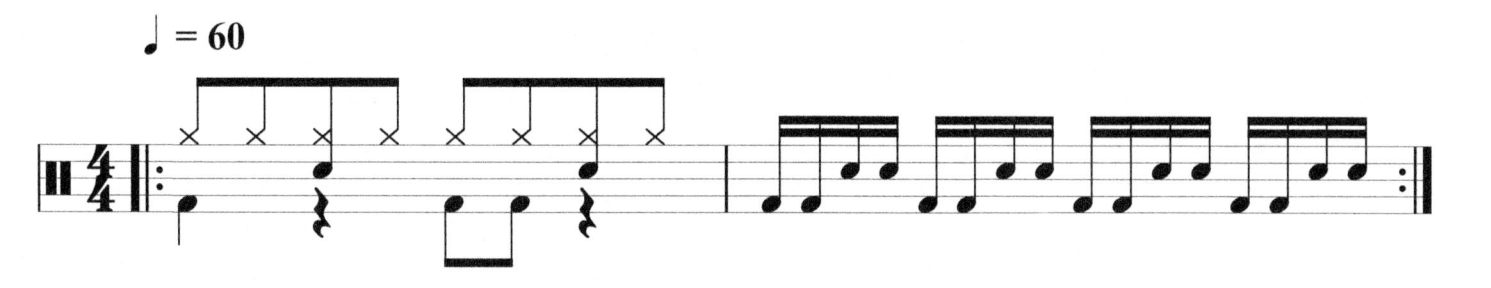

Pattern 6B

SUGGESTED LISTENING	FIVE DRUMMERS TO STUDY
• "Nomad" Black Dub	• Al Jackson Jr.
• "Jailhouse Rock" Elvis Presley	• Mona Tavakoli
• "Freed" Tracy Bonham	• Bill Bruford
• "Rolling in the Deep" Adele	• Glenn Kotche
• "Hicktown" Jason Aldean	• Matt Chamberlain

DAY 11

The work level will go up considerably through the last four days of study. Now each pattern consists of a pair of repeated two-measure phrases and the note content increases considerably, including variations on the paradiddle rudiment combinations and 16th-note groupings against the ride. These repeated patterns are to be learned as separate exercises but you could certainly play all four measures consecutively, with or without the repeats.

PATTERNS 1A–B (1:30–1:15)

We continue where we left off with 16th notes between the hands and feet, but this time the snare notes are played with one hand while you keep the hi-hat going with the other hand. This pattern flips for the next two measures (Pattern 1B).

Pattern 1A

Pattern 1B

PATTERNS 2A–B (1:15–1:00)

Now we introduce the parts of the paradiddle in pieces of each two-measure phrase.

Pattern 2A

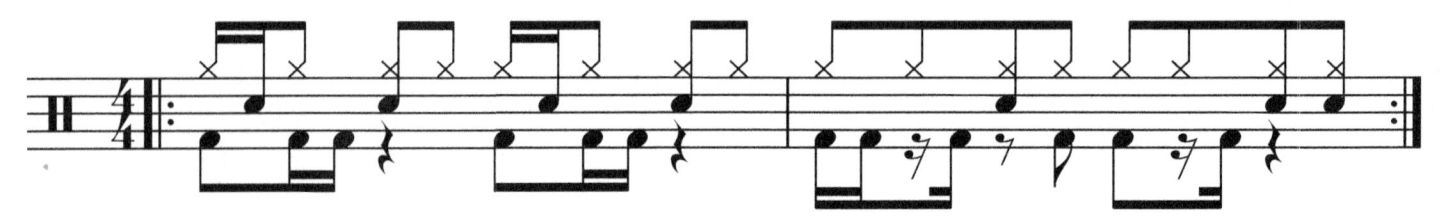

Pattern 2B

PATTERNS 3A–B (1:00–0:45)

For the first pattern, the paradiddle (measure 1) starts with the bass drum: BSBBSBSS. Then, in the second pattern, the paradiddle is reversed: SBSSBSBB. Take your time with this material, as it might be really frustrating at first. In time, however, it will open up all kinds of ways to approach the drum set.

Pattern 3A

$\downarrow = 60$

Pattern 3B

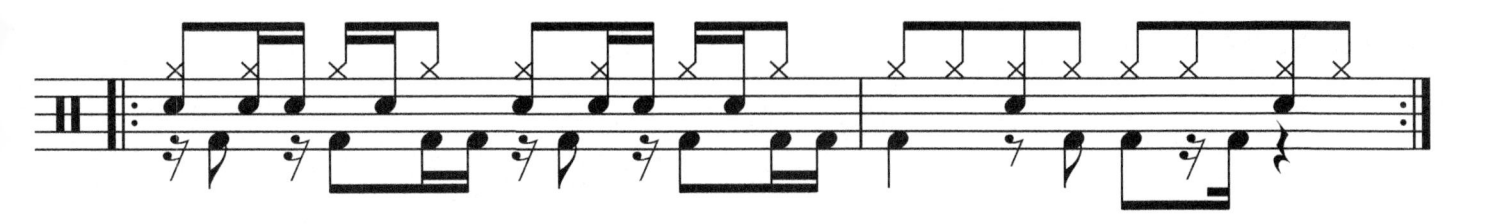

PATTERNS 4A–B (0:45–0:30)

These next two patterns take four 16th notes (between the snare and bass drum) and just move them around a bit.

Pattern 4A

$\quad\quad\quad$ ♩ = 60

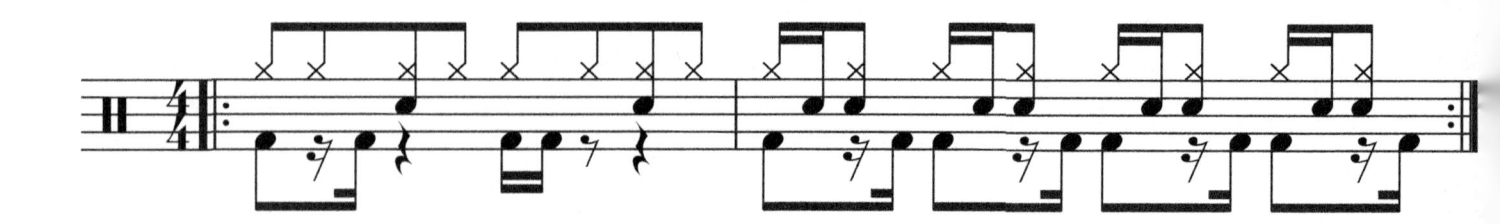

Pattern 4B

PATTERNS 5A–B (0:30–0:15)

The first pattern uses the paradiddle but with a partially open, quarter-note hi-hat. The space in measure 2 of each pattern might throw you off a bit, so keep counting!

Pattern 5A

$\quad\quad\quad$ ♩ = 60

Pattern 5B

PATTERNS 6A–B (0:15–0:00)

The last pattern of the day gives us some more paradiddle and 16th-note combos. We also move to the ride cymbal, which, by doing so, uncrosses your hands. You can move your snare hand freely around the kit once you get the rhythms sorted.

Pattern 6A

$\quad \quad \downarrow = 60$

Pattern 6B

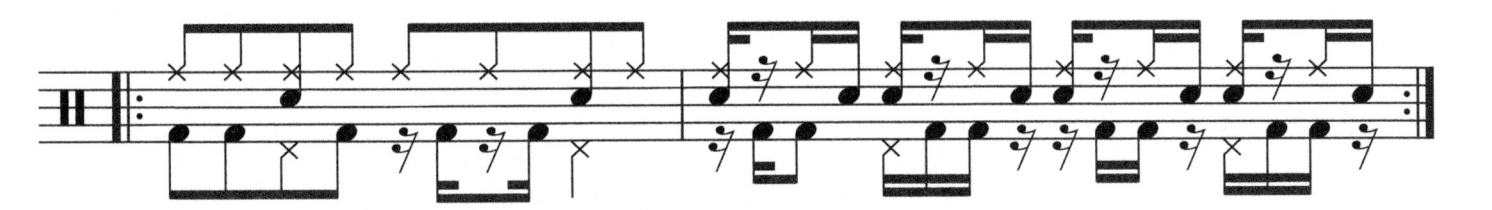

SUGGESTED LISTENING	FIVE DRUMMERS TO STUDY
• "Wicked Love" Sara Bareilles	• Roger Taylor
• "Interstate Love Song" Stone Temple Pilots	• Travis Barker
• "Island in the Sun" Weezer	• Tommy Lee
• "Take It Easy" The Eagles	• Paul Leim
• "I Sat by the Ocean" Queens of the Stone Age	• Nick Mason

DAY 12

This is where things really start to get fun. There are a lot of fill patterns here that can be played in many different ways. For the first time in the book, we notate which drums to hit during the fill because it makes learning these fills easier, but once you do learn them, you can transfer them to the rest of the kit, like we have throughout the book.

Pay close attention to the balance of sound as you strike the different surfaces and think about what the note sequences sound like when played on a single sound source. That will help you to play things more accurately. Have fun and be patient!

PATTERNS 1A–B (1:30–1:15)

We take the now-familiar "triplet-and" pattern that you played on the snare and move it around the kit. This sequence is very common in rock drumming and can be heard in many songs and in countless ways. This note grouping flows nicely when you get it down. Make sure that you complete the figure on the "and." Remember, it shouldn't sound like regular 16th notes ("1-e-&-ah"), as it's faster than that sequence. The second two-measure pattern uses a combination of both regular 16ths and triplet 16ths so you can hear the difference.

Pattern 1A

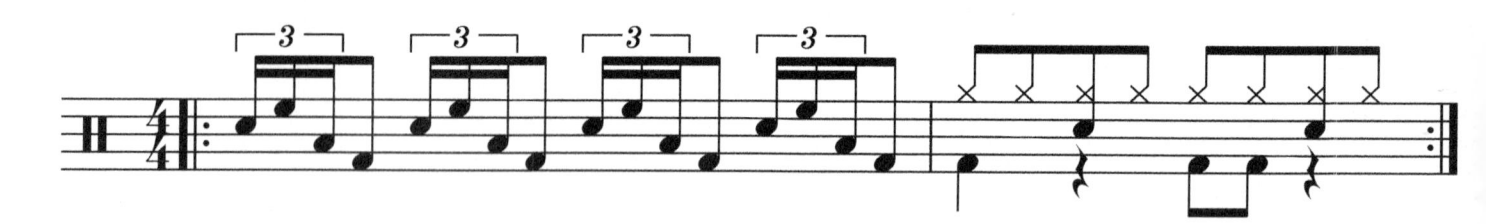

Pattern 1B

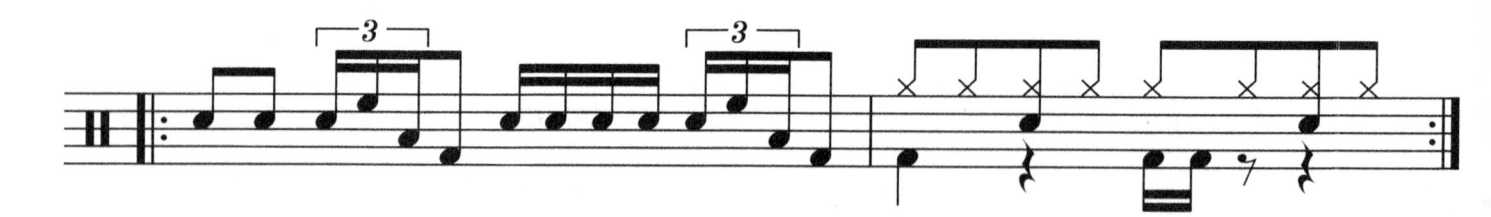

PATTERNS 2A–B (1:15–1:00)

Continuing with linear ideas, here we have regular 16ths interjected by single bass drum strikes that break up the flow of the notes in interesting ways. Of course, move these around the kit.

Pattern 2A

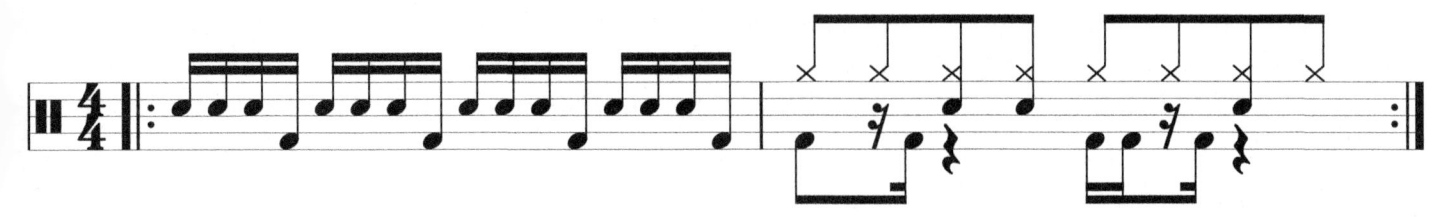

Pattern 2B

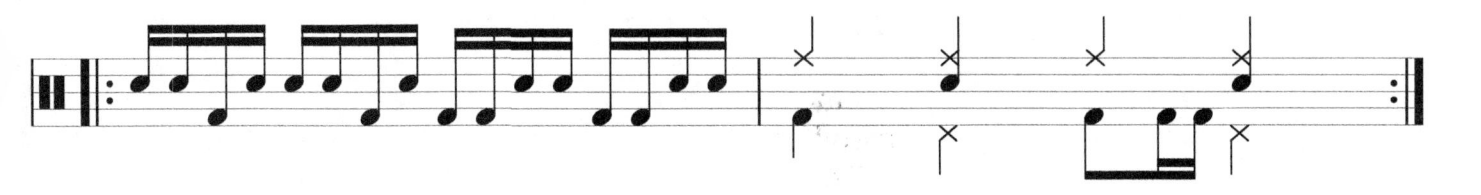

PATTERNS 3A–B (1:00–0:45)

Here, we take the 16th-note triplets (sextuplets) and place two bass-drum strikes at the end, on the fifth and sixth notes. There's a nice flow to this pattern but be sure not to rush the hands and interrupt the flow of the notes. Remember what the figure sounds like on one surface and try to emulate that.

Pattern 3A

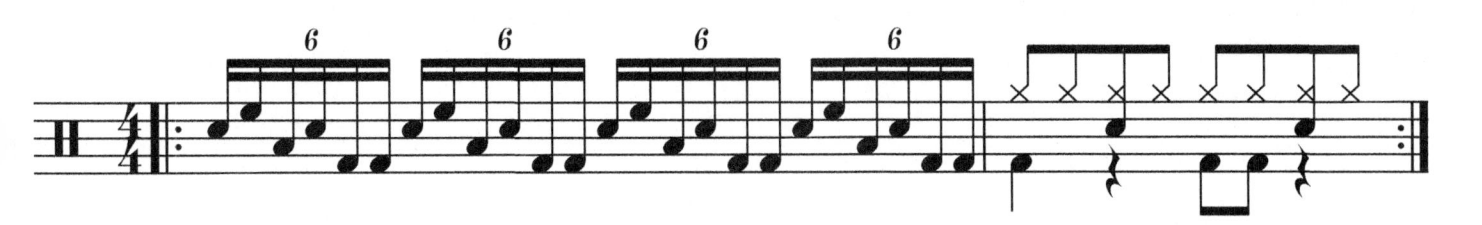

Pattern 3B

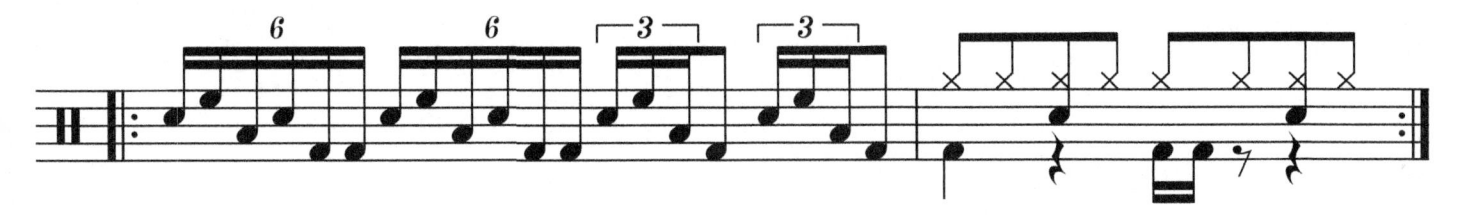

PATTERNS 4A–B (0:45–0:30)

Here are more 16th-note fills but this time distributed between the hi-hat, snare, and bass drum. I recommend that you play each sound with one limb, which will require you to play the two consecutive notes with one hand. When mastered, this can open up doors, particularly the directions in which you go around the set, keeping you from using the same sticking patterns for everything. Play the pattern as written and then move your hands to discover many new ways to play things.

Pattern 4A

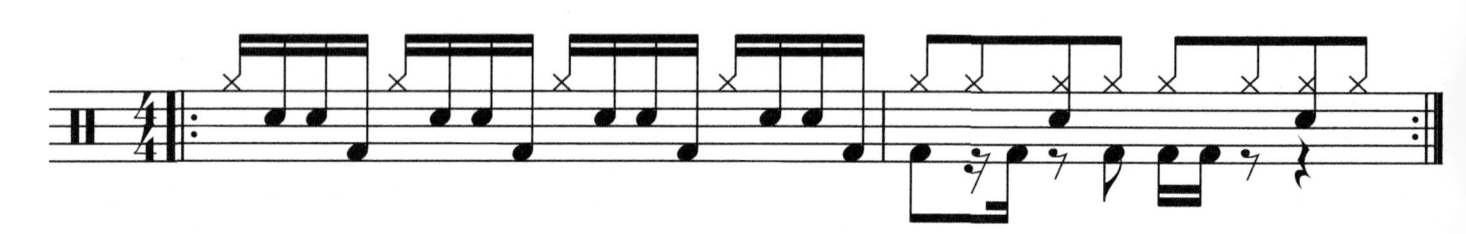

Pattern 4B

PATTERNS 5A–B (0:30–0:15)

This example is a continuation of the last pattern but with some new combinations. Use the same approach.

Pattern 5A

Pattern 5B

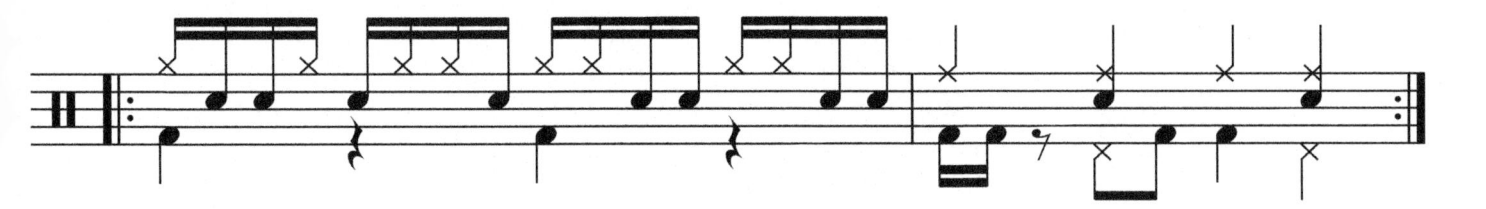

PATTERNS 6A–B (0:15–0:00)

The last pattern of the day introduces another linear sextuplet figure. This time, each hand plays one note, with the bass drum playing the third note of each triplet. Make sure to play the second note a bit softer in the pattern, which will help to keep it consistent. Then move the hands about the kit.

Pattern 6A

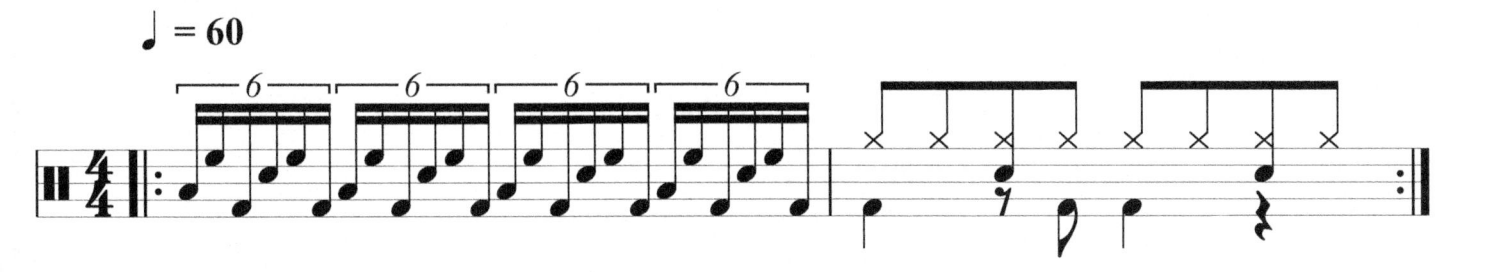

Pattern 6B

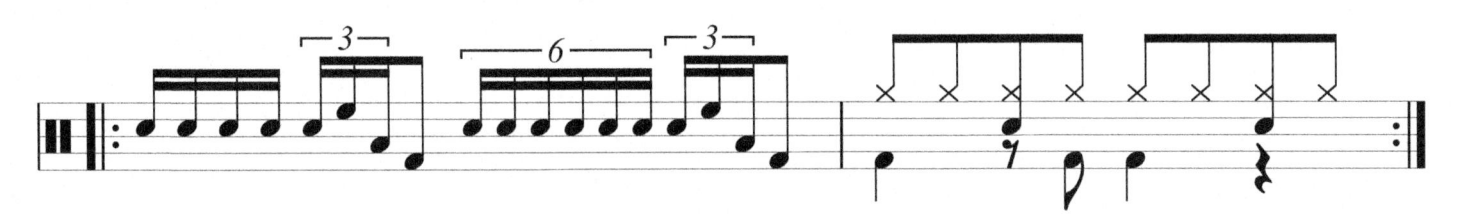

SUGGESTED LISTENING	FIVE DRUMMERS TO STUDY
• "Fame" David Bowie	• Mark Guiliana
• "Sledgehammer" Peter Gabriel	• Dennis Davis
• "Best I Can" Rush	• Daru Jones
• "Subterranean Homesick Blues" Bob Dylan	• Will Calhoun
• "Out of My Hands" Jason Mraz	• Dave Grohl

DAY 13

For the next six patterns, we open the hi-hat on the "and" of every beat. Hi-hat opens are common in a number of forms of music, so it's important to get some coordination developed in that area. As usual, take your time and, if a pattern is difficult for you, then feel free to simplify it by playing less notes or by taking it in pieces (adding one limb at a time).

PATTERNS 1A–B (1:30–1:15)

Here, we combine quarter notes, eighth notes, and rests.

Pattern 1A

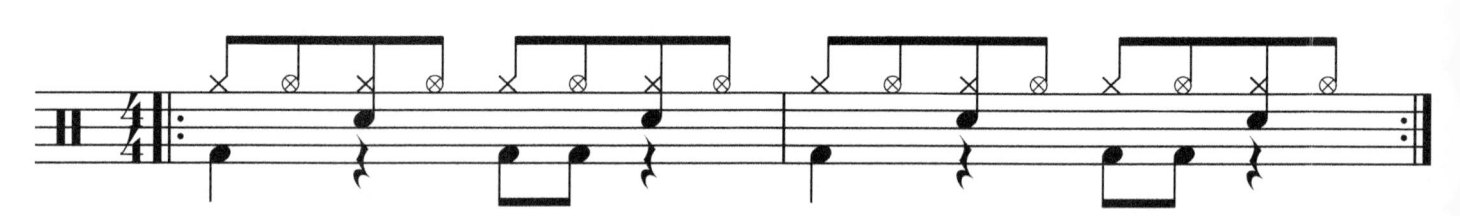

Pattern 1B

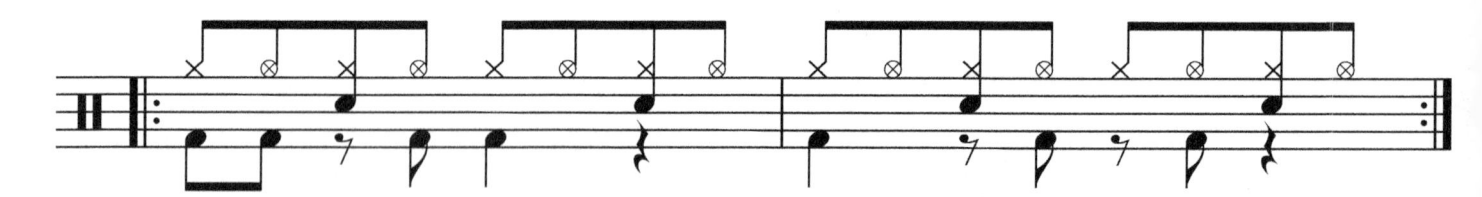

PATTERNS 2A–B (1:15–1:00)

Sixteenth-note combinations are used here in the bass drum. These patterns might get a bit tricky, so be patient.

Pattern 2A

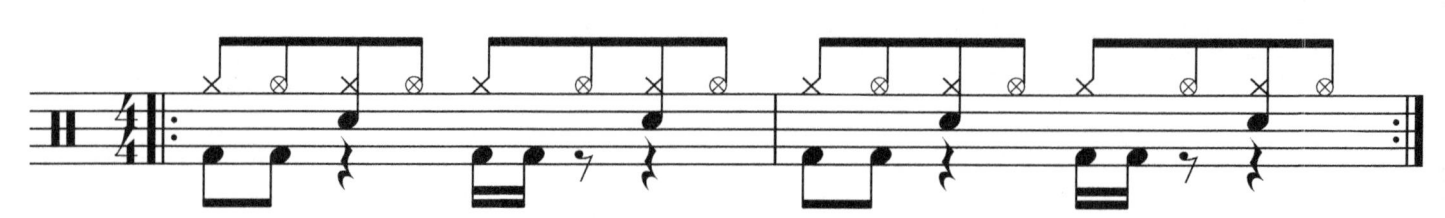

Pattern 2B

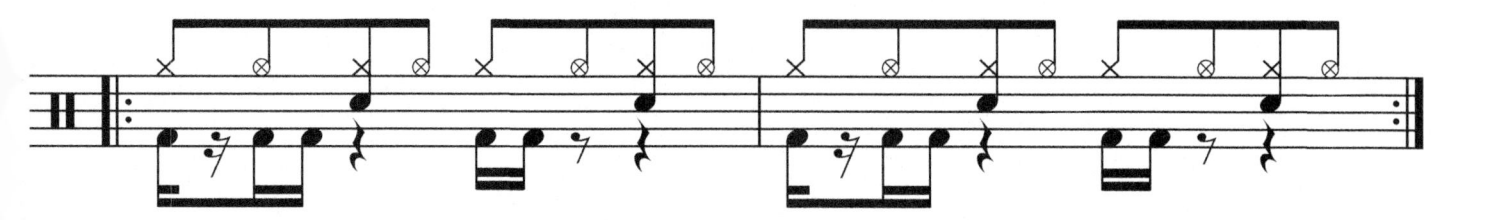

PATTERNS 3A–B (1:00–0:45)

These patterns feature more 16th- and eighth-note groupings, with each measure changing content.

Pattern 3A

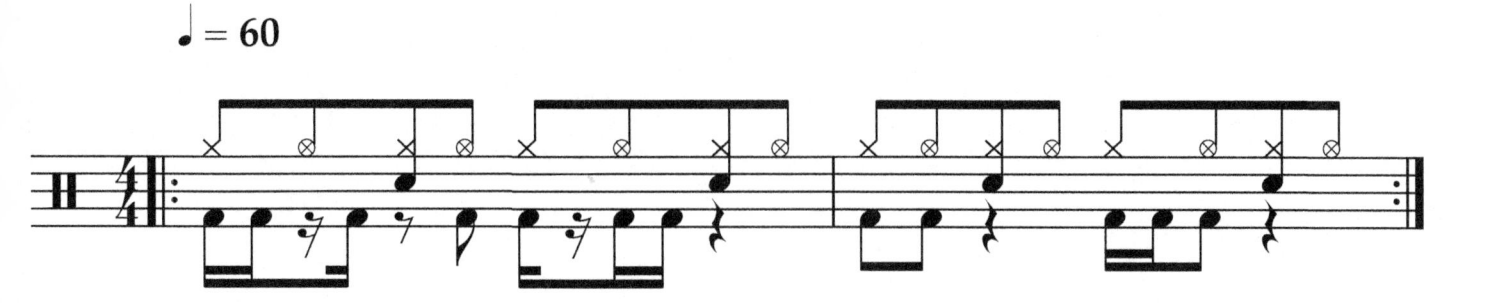

Pattern 3B

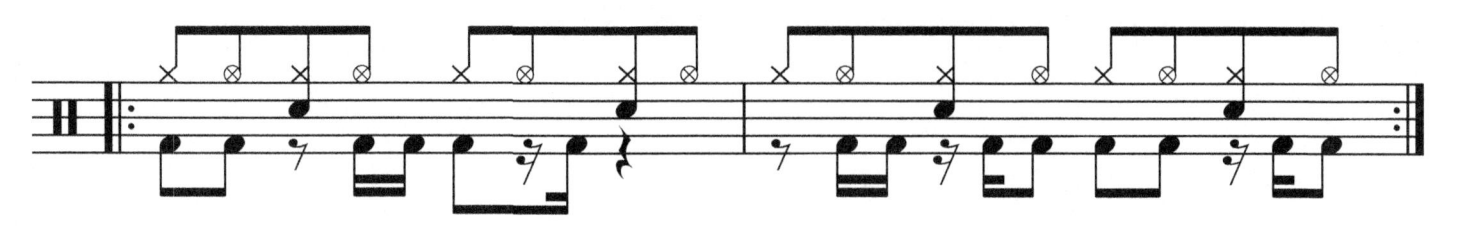

PATTERNS 4A–B (0:45–0:30)

The hand-and-foot paradiddle shows up again in this pattern.

Pattern 4A

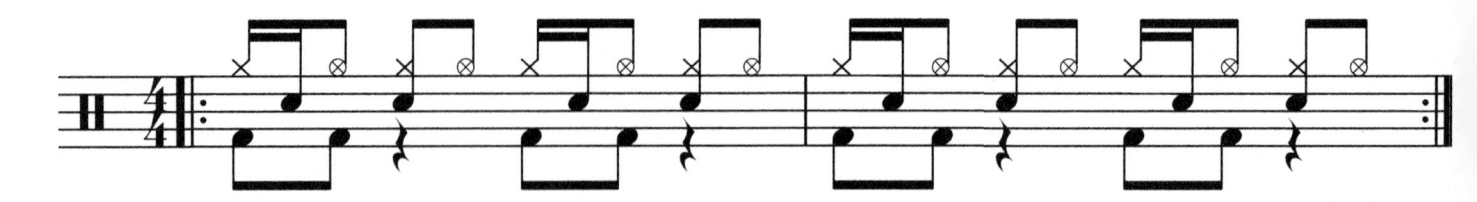

Pattern 4B

PATTERNS 5A–B (0:30–0:15)

Picking up the tempo a bit (90 BPM), these next sequences ride on the floor tom and then the rack tom, which is a common change-up in rock drumming.

Pattern 5A

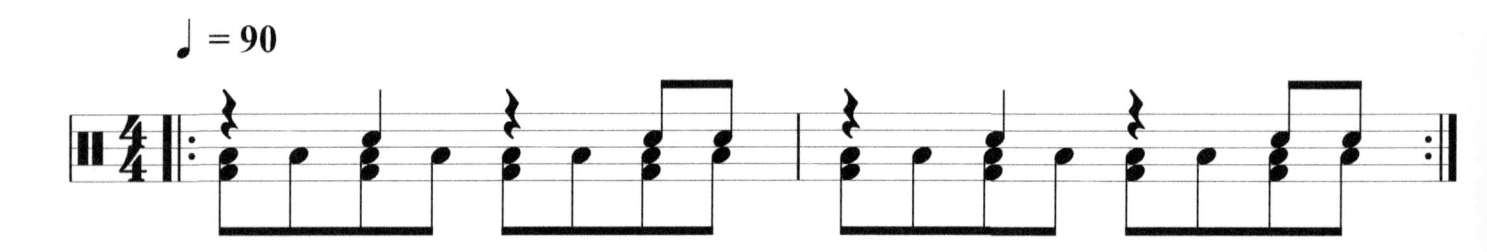

Pattern 5B

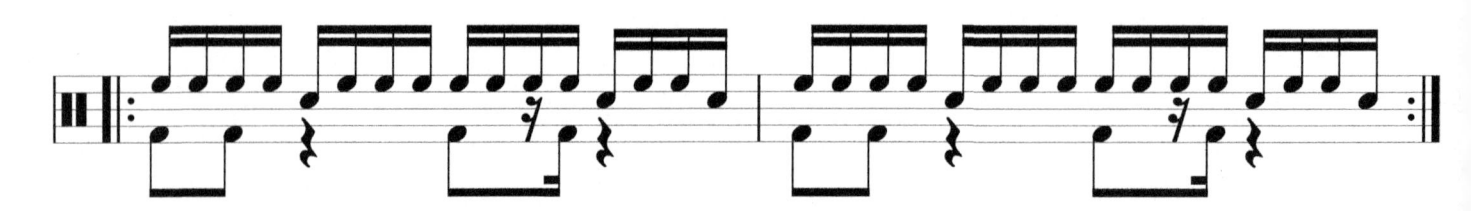

PATTERNS 6A–B (0:15–0:00)

This pattern alternates floor tom and bass drum for a double-bass-type groove. Watch the balance of your hands and foot on this pattern so it sounds even.

Pattern 6A

Our last paradiddle variation for today alternates between the hi-hat and snare while the bass drum plays various combinations of notes. When you're ready, you can move both hands around the kit to find lots of interesting ways to play these notes. Have fun with it!

Pattern 6B

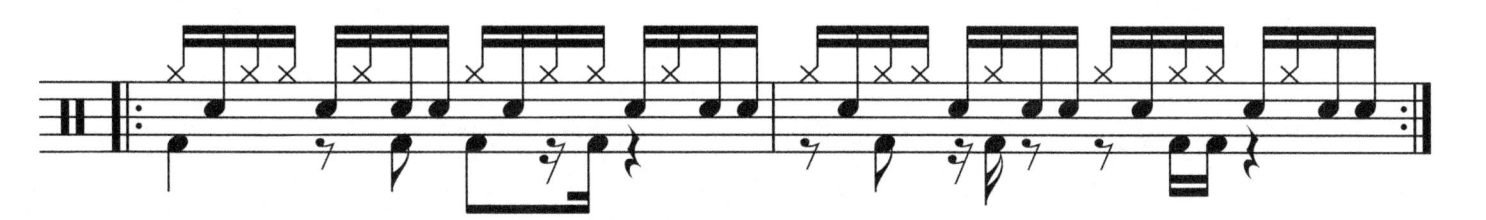

SUGGESTED LISTENING	FIVE DRUMMERS TO STUDY
• "Heart of Glass" Blondie	• Omar Hakim
• "Uninvisible" Medeski, Martin & Wood	• Jojo Mayer
• "Crosstown Traffic" Jimi Hendrix	• Danny Carey
• "It's Too Funky in Here" James Brown	• Brian Blade
• "Prisoner" Miley Cyrus	• Steve Smith

DAY 14

We wrap things up with a mixed bag of patterns that touch on a number of different approaches that will enable you to branch off to styles that extend beyond rock drums. We'll mix up hi-hat opens, as well as add some grace notes, accents, and a couple of foot ostinato patterns and EDM-type grooves.

PATTERNS 1A–B (1:30–1:15)

Here are two different types of EDM-style grooves that keep the bass drum going for all four beats and include some mixed snare combinations and 16th notes on the hi-hat.

Pattern 1A

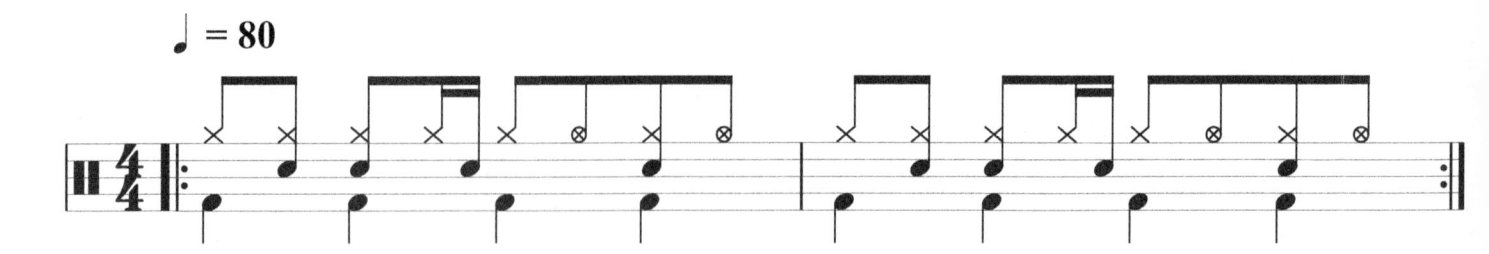

Pattern 1B

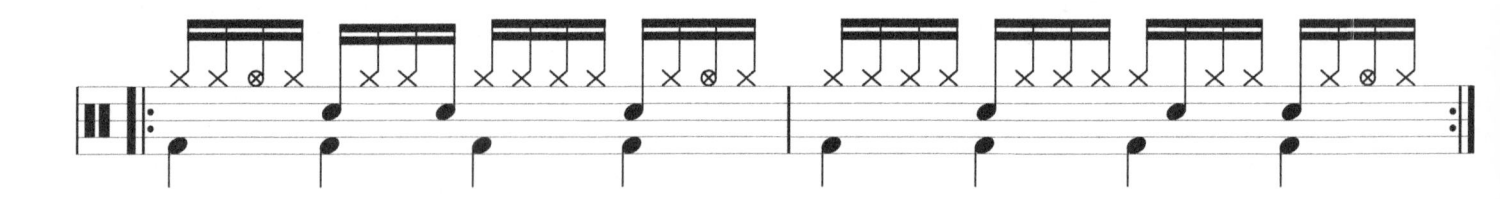

PATTERNS 2A–B (1:15–1:00)

Here's a rock-style triplet groove with partially opened hi-hats.

Pattern 2A

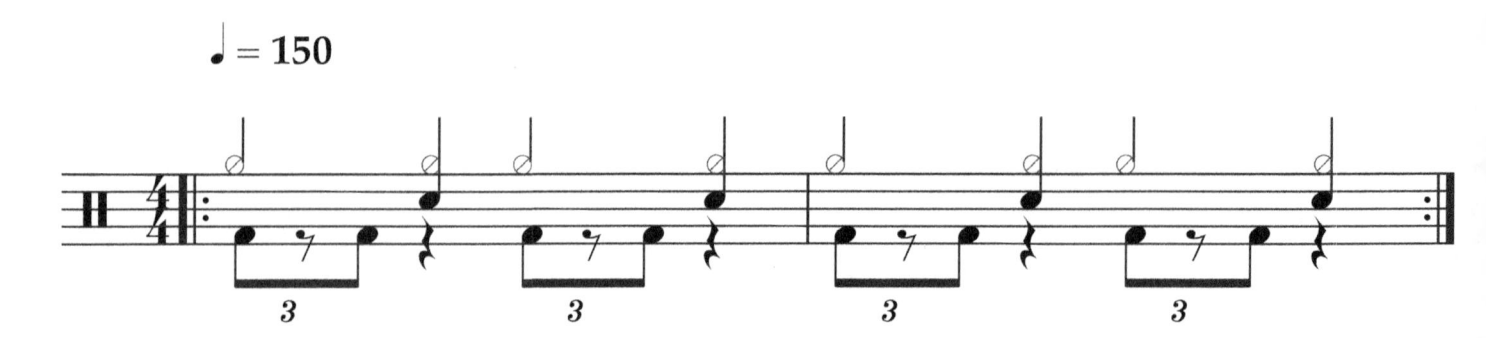

Pattern 2B

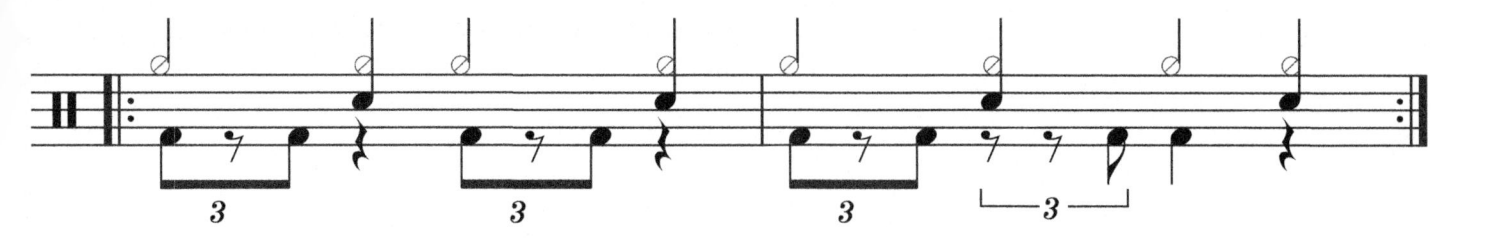

PATTERNS 3A–B (1:00–0:45)

Partially opened hi-hats, ghost notes on the snare, and accents on beats 2 and 4 make this a challenging set of notes. As a general rule, keep the tip of the stick close to the drum for the ghost notes, and higher for the accents. Listen to the audio to get an idea of how the patterns should sound.

Pattern 3A

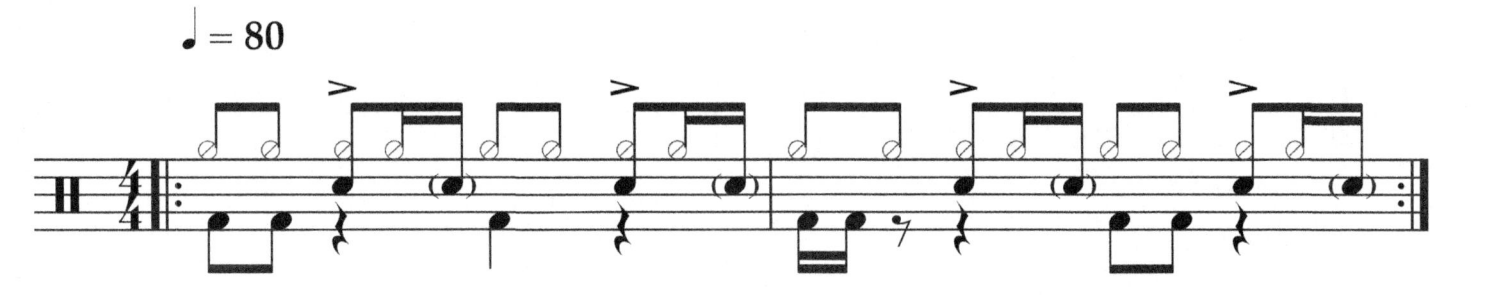

Pattern 3B

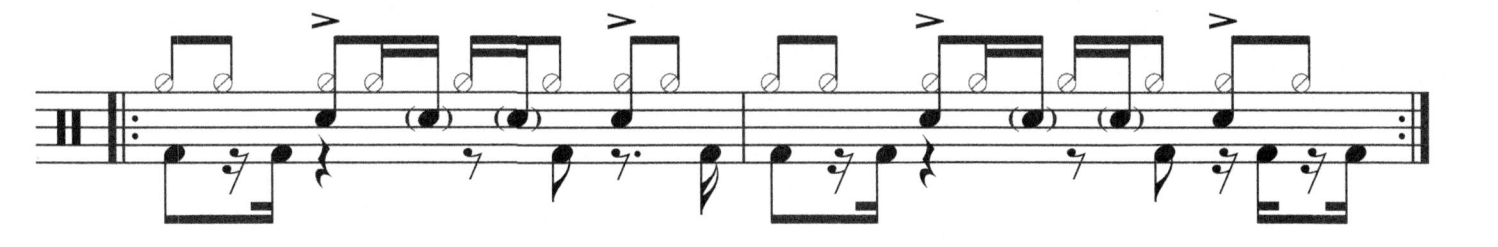

PATTERNS 4A–B (0:45–0:30)

Here, we play more ghost notes and accents, but this time with a quarter-note hi-hat pattern. These types of grooves are very common in rock and can be performed many different ways—this is just the tip of the iceberg.

Pattern 4A

Pattern 4B

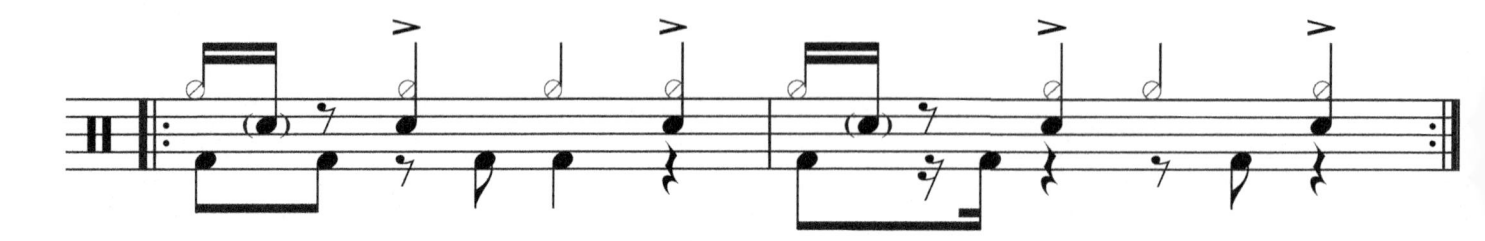

PATTERNS 5A–B (0:30–0:15)

As you near the end of the material, we add some weak-side ostinato coordination work. The hi-hat is closed with your foot on the "ands" of every beat (measure 1), which will be new for you and challenging. Working on your weaker limbs will improve your overall dexterity and confidence on the drums, but be sure you're doing things correctly, as it's common for limbs to follow one another when working on these types of patterns.

Pattern 5A

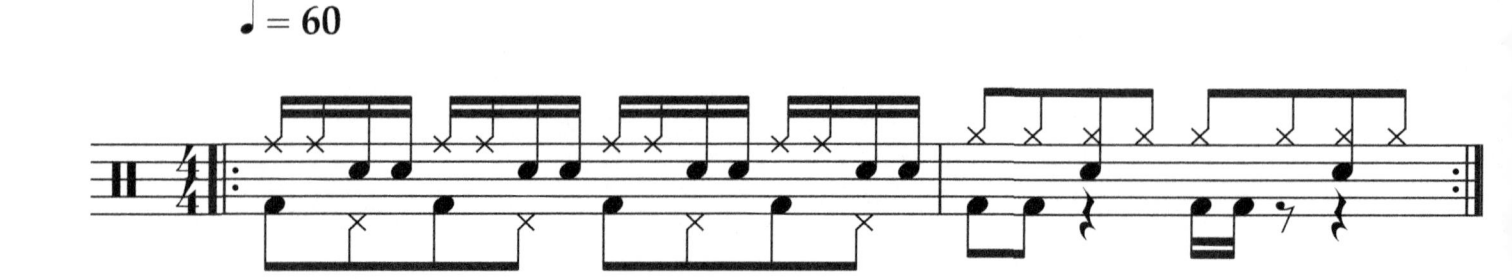

Pattern 5B

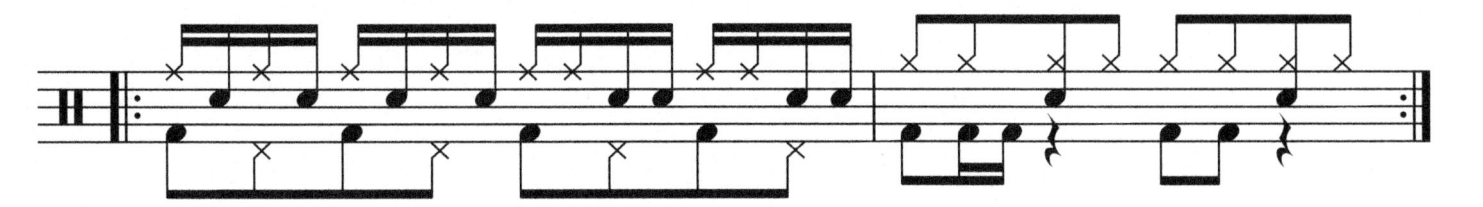

PATTERNS 6A–B (0:15–0:00)

The last pattern in the series features more ostinato work and applies some familiar sticking patterns. Like much of the material, when you feel comfortable, move your hands to different surfaces and push yourself to maintain consistency with the foot patterns, all while keeping everything sounding balanced. There are so many ways to develop this material, so I encourage you to explore other methods and concepts.

Pattern 6A

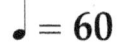

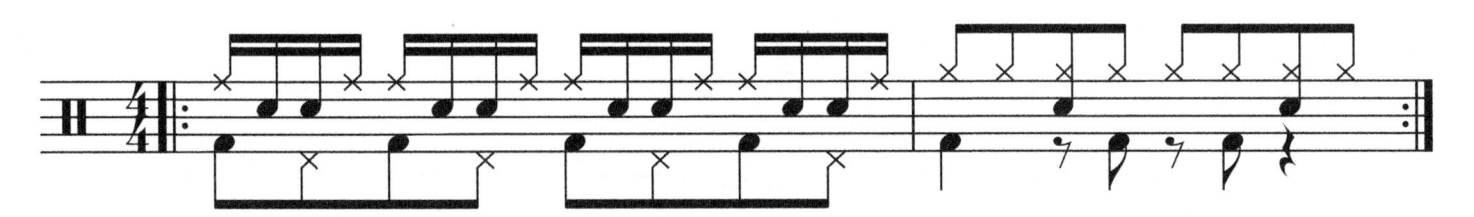

Pattern 6B

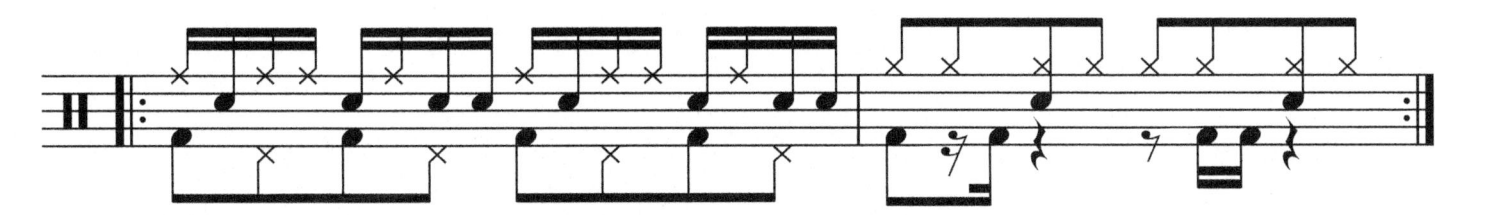

SUGGESTED LISTENING	FIVE DRUMMERS TO STUDY
• "Blinding Lights" The Weeknd	• Aynsley Dunbar
• "Hold On" Alabama Shakes	• Terry Bozzio
• "Come As You Are" Nirvana	• Rick Marotta
• "Give It Away" Red Hot Chili Peppers	• Gregg Bissonette
• "Black Hole Sun" Soundgarden	• John "JR" Robinson

BONUS EXERCISES

Here are two bonus exercises that are a cross section of the material in this book, arranged in pseudo song form, to help you improve your music-reading skills. Both exercises are 16 bars long (including the repeats) and use material from various sections of the book, so nothing is brand new here. The tempos are only suggested—you can, of course, play the exercises at whatever pace works best for you. As you work through the material, watch out for the repeated sections. Most of all, have fun!

EXERCISE 1

$\quad \downarrow = 80$

EXERCISE 2

♩ = 90

MOVING FORWARD

Congratulations! You made it! I sincerely hope you enjoyed this process and were able to benefit from it, whatever the rate you worked through this material at. There is *so* much wonderful music to experience and enjoy in this world, and hopefully you've discovered some new music along the way.

Additionally, you should have a handle on some of the coordinations required to learn and play music that appeals to you. The "rock" music world is vast and all-encompassing, really. It doesn't take much to slide into a new style and adapt the elements in this book to the new styles you discover. The key is to have an open mind. If you're searching for more, please have a look at my genre-focused book *Drum Set 365* (available at Amazon), which covers over 15 different styles of music. Finally, if you have any questions about the material in this book or anything in the music business, I would love to hear from you! You can contact me through my website: *daveschoepke.com*.

Happy drumming!

ABOUT THE AUTHOR

Dave Schoepke hails from the Greater Milwaukee area. He has been a professional recording and touring musician for three decades, including treks across North America and Europe. His credits include Jethro Tull guitarist Martin Barre and songsmith Willy Porter. He has been a creative force in Willy's band since 2002.

An active session musician with appearances on over 50 albums, Dave does remote recording from his home studio for artists worldwide. He appears on the recordings of such diverse artists as Bryan Lee, Darrell Scott, Natalia Zukerman, Raining Jane, Billy Flynn, Doug Woolverton, Victor DeLorenzo, Michael Bettine, Russ Johnson, Todd Sickafoose, Brian Ritchie, Chuck Garrick, Allison Miller, Ray Bonneville, Paul Cebar, and Alan Thomson. Dave also appears on over a dozen instructional CDs for Hal Leonard, covering many genres.

His solo drums project has produced three all-drums albums and garnered acclaimed reviews from *Modern Drummer*, *Recording Magazine*, and numerous online music critics around the world. The 400th issue of *Recording Magazine* includes a multi-page feature on Dave's process of writing and recording his album *Drums on Low*.

Dave has been teaching drums for over 30 years and has done numerous clinics and educational-based symposiums with legendary artists Jeff Coffin, Ed Thigpen, Paul Wertico, Dom Famularo, Gregg Bissonette, and Carmine Appice. He maintains a busy schedule of teaching, touring, clinics, and sessions and is always striving to evolve in every facet of his music-making. For lesson inquiries or questions, Dave can be reached via his website, *daveschoepke.com*.

Printed in Great Britain
by Amazon